T0386154

THE NEW NANCY

Encapsulations: Critical Comics Studies

The New Nancy

Flexible and Relatable Daily Comics
in the Twenty-First Century

JEFF KARNICKY

UNIVERSITY OF NEBRASKA PRESS   LINCOLN

The University of Nebraska Press is part of a land-grant
    institution with campuses and programs on the past,
    present, and future homelands of the Pawnee, Ponca,
    Otoe-Missouria, Omaha, Dakota, Lakota, Kaw,
    Cheyenne, and Arapaho Peoples, as well as those of the
    relocated Ho-Chunk, Sac and Fox, and Iowa Peoples.

Library of Congress Cataloging-in-Publication Data
Names: Karnicky, Jeffrey, author.
Title: The new Nancy: flexible and relatable daily comics
    in the twenty-first century / Jeff Karnicky.
Description: Lincoln: University of Nebraska Press,
    [2023] | Series: Encapsulations: critical comics studies |
    Includes bibliographical references and index.
Identifiers: LCCN 2022056857
ISBN 9781496235862 (paperback)
ISBN 9781496237194 (epub)
ISBN 9781496237200 (pdf)
Subjects: LCSH: Comic books, strips, etc.—United
    States—History and criticism. | Mass media—United
    States—History—21st century. | Jaimes, Olivia.
    Nancy (Comic strip) | BISAC: SOCIAL SCIENCE /
    Media Studies | LITERARY CRITICISM / Comics
    & Graphic Novels | LCGFT: Comics criticism.
Classification: LCC PN6725 .K38 2023 | DDC
    741.5/973—dc23/eng/20230418
LC record available at https://lccn.loc.gov/2022056857

Set and designed in Minion by N. Putens.

To Max

CONTENTS

ILLUSTRATIONS

SERIES EDITORS' INTRODUCTION

Martin Lund and Julia Round

In *The New Nancy*, Jeff Karnicky closely analyses Olivia Jaimes's rebooted version of this daily comic strip, building on the work of previous theorists to identify and define the concepts of flexibility and relatability and to explore how they drive the success of this comic. By investigating how Jaimes reshapes this classic legacy strip into a flexible and relatable model for daily webcomics, while drawing attention to the ways in which the cartoonist foregrounds her own creative process and struggles for legitimacy, Karnicky builds an argument that engages with comics production and consumption in today's world. It highlights how comics creators must not just craft a text but also present their own processes and personas to audiences and how the dynamics between creators and consumers rest on shared understandings and relatability. These transactions take place across multiple platforms and formats, and Karnicky shows how these changing material conditions also affect the production and reception of comics today.

This discussion has much to offer in a postpandemic world where creative practice and other ways of working continue to take place in hybrid digital and physical spaces. It questions what happens when traditional publishing formats and readerships change and explores the ways that comics stories can foreground this by playing with spaces both within and outside panels. These sorts of questions of change and evolution are key to comics studies, and engaging with them is one of the aims of this series. In the creation of comics or graphic novels, "encapsulation" refers to the artistic and cognitive process whereby panels, images, words, and page layout create meaning and engage the reader. These connotations of selection and design underpin the aims of Encapsulations. Our series of short monographs offers close readings of carefully delineated bodies of comics work, with an emphasis on expanding the critical range and depth of comics studies.

By looking at understudied and overlooked texts, artists, and publishers, Encapsulations facilitates a move away from the same "big" and oft-examined texts. Instead, the series uses more diverse case studies to explore new and existing critical theories in tune with an interdisciplinary, intersectional, and global approach to comics scholarship. With an eye to breaking established patterns and forging new opportunities for scholarship, books in this series advance the theoretical grounding of comics scholarship and broaden critical knowledge of global comics. By showcasing new interdisciplinary perspectives and addressing emerging conceptual, formal, and methodological problems, Encapsulations promotes new approaches, contributes to the diversity of comics scholarship, and delves into uncharted sections of the comics archive.

Compact, affordable, and accessibly written, books in the Encapsulations series are addressed to the interested general reader as well as scholars and students. These volumes provide teachable, critical texts that foster a deeper general understanding of comics' cultural and historical impact, promote critical public literacy, and expand notions of what's worthy of academic study. We are delighted to welcome *The New Nancy*'s contribution to this field.

ACKNOWLEDGMENTS

I thank Julia Round and Martin Lund, who offered me superb editorial guidance as I worked on this book. Aaron Kashtan's careful reading and helpful suggestions helped immensely. Likewise, I thank the anonymous reader, whose report aided the revision process. Thank you to Jeremy T. Hall for scrupulous copy editing. As I've said previously, without Jeff Nealon's and Rich Doyle's instruction at Penn State (long ago), this book would not have been possible. I cannot thank Megan Brown enough for her love and support (and proofreading). I wrote most of this book during the pandemic, and I thank Suki and Pippa for being my companion species while I was working.

My son, Max, is an excellent research assistant, and I dedicate this book to him (even if he thinks he can beat me at Charlie Brown trivia).

THE NEW NANCY

1. *Nancy*, by Olivia Jaimes, April 9, 2018. NANCY © 2018. Reprinted by permission of ANDREWS MCMEEL SYNDICATION for UFS. All rights reserved.

Introduction
"Going *In* on That Cornbread"

Becoming Flexible, Becoming #Relatable (April 9, 2018)

Daily newspaper comics in the United States have fallen on hard times in the twenty-first century. Long gone are the days of the early twentieth century, when William Randolph Hearst and Joseph Pulitzer fought bidding wars over cartoonists like Richard Outcault and Frederic Opper.[1] Gone, too, are the twentieth-century comic strips that could help drive newspaper sales, including Charles Schulz's *Peanuts*, Chic Young's *Blondie*, and Mort Walker's *Beetle Bailey*.[2] Print newspaper circulation and revenue have fallen precipitously. U.S. newspaper circulation in 2018 reached its lowest point since 1940 and is down by over 50 percent since 1985. Newspaper revenue declined 62 percent between 2008 and 2018.[3] As newspapers cut costs, the small space given to comic strips continues to shrink. In short, daily newspaper comics have lost much of their cultural impact.

In turn, the field of American and anglophone comics studies has tended to favor studies of graphic novels and superhero comics and to neglect daily comics. Charles Hatfield, in his influential *Alternative Comics: An Emerging Literature*, argues that newspaper comics, precisely because of their shrinking space, have lost their relevance: "The fact is that the age of the large format newspaper strip passed decades ago. Though some artists have adapted well to the smaller format, strips continue to be cramped by unyielding editorial policies."[4] Hatfield argues that newspaper comics have become conservative and static because of these editorial policies and that they have thus lost much of the cultural capital they held in the past. He writes, "The newspaper page tends to remain within its predictable bounds, with little change, year after year. Thus comics in the short form are, by and large, severely hobbled in terms of graphic and thematic potential."[5] In his argument for the creative and literary merits of long-form alternative comics, Hatfield sacrifices the daily newspaper comic as a form that has lost these merits.

Nevertheless, daily newspaper comics persist. Creators and syndicates have adapted to their reduced circumstances by moving online and rethinking the ways that daily comics connect with readers. King Features Syndicate's Comics Kingdom and Andrews McMeel Universal's GoComics offer free daily comics online. Comics Kingdom offers more than sixty daily syndicated newspaper comics, and GoComics provides access to hundreds of syndicated newspaper comics and webcomics. Nearly every comic that appears in a U.S. daily newspaper can be read on one of these two sites.[6] Thanks to this access, daily newspaper comics are now better thought of as hybrids that appear both in print and online. Aaron Kashtan, in his 2019 book, *Between Pen and Pixel: Comics, Materiality, and the Book of the Future*, calls such comics "flexible." He writes that "readers value the unique properties of both print and digital, and this has resulted in an environment where print and digital modes of delivery have worked to support rather than replace each other."[7] It has become increasingly common for comics to exist in both print and digital forms at once. I want to push Kashtan's argument, as it relates to daily comic strips, in two directions.

First, I argue that daily comics have adapted to this new environment by becoming flexible beyond just their ability to appear in print or digitally. Contemporary, flexible daily comics embrace the material elements of comic production and consumption in their strips. Creators emphasize the actual labor of producing comics, which importantly includes much more than drawing and writing. The work of producing comics often includes building a brand, selling merchandise, and working multiple jobs to earn a living wage. Flexible comics can be commented on, the moment they are posted online; this instant feedback has altered the relationship between readers and creators. The changing media environment of daily comics has altered both their form and their content. I want to be clear here that the material conditions surrounding comics' production have always influenced the form and content of comics. The larger culture in which comic strips have been produced has always shaped and been shaped by comics, just as comics have always been shaped by and helped to shape the prevalent ideologies of their day. Daily comics' flexibility connects to the changing nature of work today, as comic creation has become part of the gig economy and can rarely be seen as the lucrative career it sometimes was in the twentieth century. Like many forms of work today, comic creation is precarious. Workers in the field lack financial security even if they have a syndicate contract. While "precarity" and "flexibility" are not necessarily synonyms, they share some meaning. Precarity can be seen as the more ominous side of flexibility. Flexibility might promise a certain amount of freedom to do as one pleases, while precarity offers a reminder of the dangers of unstable work. Flexible daily comics often consider their own precarity as they reflect on their own creation.

Second, I argue that daily comic creators have to work to form a #relatable connection between themselves and readers. Connections with readers have changed immensely from the days when fans could mail a letter to a creator and hope to get a reply. Most contemporary comic creators cultivate an online persona through which they engage readers. Creators must have a sense of who their readers are and what their readers know. Based on this understanding, creators form a relationship with their readers. Thus, a creator and their work become relatable to readers with specific identities, beliefs, and expectations. Like flexibility, relatability can be precarious. Cultivating a connection with readers with multiple identities and expectations might form a strong, mutually beneficial bond that results in a successful daily comic strip. But relatability can become fraught, toxic, and sometimes even dangerous. I want to be clear here—just as comics have always been immersed in the material and ideological conditions of their times, creators have always had to pay attention to what they believe readers want. In the twentieth century, this relationship was defined broadly by letters to the editors of newspapers, mailed correspondence, and the number of newspapers that carried a syndicated strip. As comics have become flexible, their connection to readers has altered significantly. Becoming #relatable, as I will discuss below, means much more than just being aware of one's readers. Maintaining relatability requires constant work for creators.

In the next two sections of this introduction, I will refine the terms "flexible" and "#relatable" as they apply to contemporary comics. I will focus on Olivia Jaimes's 2018 reboot of the classic *Nancy* comic strip as a particularly flexible and #relatable daily comic that lives comfortably in both print and digital formats. Jaimes's *Nancy* makes the changing roles of publishers, creators, and readers a part of the strip itself. *Nancy* can be read as a model for what daily comics in the twenty-first century can do to remain culturally and socially relevant in a world where the means of production and consumption are under constant revision.

Becoming flexible fundamentally changes the economic and cultural space of daily comics. As newspaper readership shrinks, the cultural space of daily comics does too. Flexible twenty-first-century comics must work to gain and keep readers in quite different ways than twentieth-century newspaper strips did. Like many forms of work in the twenty-first century, the job of comic creator has become precarious, especially in comparison to how comic creators worked in the twentieth century.

In the second half of the twentieth century, a small number of mostly white, mostly male comics creators were able to make their living writing a daily comic strip. Charles Schulz serves as the exemplar here. He published a *Peanuts* strip every single day from October 2, 1950, to January 3, 2000, with his Sunday strip running until February 13, 2000. While Schulz's consistency stands out, he was not alone in making a career of comic strip creation. Ernie Bushmiller wrote *Nancy* from 1938 until his death in 1982. Chic Young made a living from *Blondie* from 1930 until his death in 1973. In 1948 *Blondie* was syndicated in 1,136 daily newspapers, and Young's yearly salary was $300,000.[8] Mort Walker created *Beetle Bailey* in 1950 and *Hi and Lois* in 1954, making a living off both strips until his death in 2018. Daily comic strip writing was a lucrative field for a multitude of creators between roughly 1950 and 2000, with many creators writing strips until their death. Even after the creator's death, many of these strips stayed in their family as legacy strips. Chic Young's sons took over *Blondie*; Jeff Keane took over *Family Circus* from his father Bill Keane; and Mort Walker's sons continued *Hi and Lois*, to note just a few examples. In short, in post–World War II America, comics creator was the kind of career that seems to exist less and less today: a well-paying, secure job that could sometimes be passed from generation to generation. While the number of creators who were able to follow this career path was obviously quite low, it promised stability and a middle-class lifestyle for those who produced a syndicated comic strip.[9]

In mid-twentieth-century America, the overwhelming majority of syndicated newspaper cartoon creators were white men. A few white women made a living as creators of soap-operatic comic strips, most notably Dale Messick, who wrote and drew *Brenda Starr* from 1940 to 1980. Black creators were rarely given access to the comic pages of mainstream newspapers. Instead, they turned to Black newspapers, most notably the *Pittsburgh Courier*, to publish comics. Frances Gateward and John Jennings note that the *Courier* "could boast of having editions in fourteen major cities and a readership of over one million" in the late 1940s.[10] The *Courier* had a comics page that, as Nancy Goldstein writes, included "two single panels on the left side . . . and five or six cartoonists' strips on the right."[11] Oliver Harrington's single-panel *Dark Laughter*, originally created for the *Amsterdam News*, was published in the *Courier*.[12] Goldstein writes that Harrington "has been called the Michelangelo of black-press cartoonists."[13] Perhaps more notably, between 1937 and 1956, the *Courier* published "four different comic strips and cartoons" by Jackie Ormes, who is "considered to be the first African American woman newspaper cartoonist."[14] In writing of Ormes in 2013, Goldstein notes that her work, like that of other mid-twentieth-century Black cartoonists, was long "invisible" to scholars. "Until recently," Goldstein writes, "Black newspapers were not considered part of the accepted canon of comics history, a lapse of inclusion that some critics might identify as racial prejudice."[15] Goldstein points out that the original copies of Black newspapers have mostly been destroyed and that the microfilmed images that exist "often appear blotchy, distorted, or scratched, corrupting the crisp lines and clear space created by cartoonists like

Ormes."[16] This archival neglect and until-recent exclusion from the canon of comic scholarship, taken together with the gate-keeping that kept Black creators from publishing in mainstream white American newspapers, highlights the systemic racism that kept the comics pages white through the 1950s. As comic critic Jeet Heer writes, complaints from Black readers in the 1940s about racial caricatures on the comic page helped lead to "the disappearance of offensive stereotypes."[17] But instead of being replaced "by non-racist Black characters (who might have offended racist White readers) . . . the comics sections of the 1950s became very lily-white, with far fewer non-White characters than before."[18]

Creators such as Young, Brown, Keane, and Schulz, whose work filled the "lily-white" comic pages of those days, clearly benefited from the exclusion of artists and writers who were not white males. As I am focusing on the reboot of *Nancy*, a brief consideration of Ernie Bushmiller's professional life can show how he be benefitted from the gender and racial prejudices of his day to get a start in comics. Following this discussion of Bushmiller, I will describe Olivia Jaimes's path to becoming the new *Nancy* creator in 2018. The contrast between Bushmiller's and Jaimes's working lives serves to highlight many of the differences between twentieth- and twenty-first-century comic creation.

Ernie Bushmiller began his career doing hackwork like drawing crossword puzzles and illustrating brain teasers at the *New York World* newspaper. Bushmiller, thanks to the connections he formed at the *World*, was able to publish his first comic when he was fifteen. After serving as an apprentice for a few years, Bushmiller took over the daily strip *Fritzi Ritz* in 1925. He introduced Fritzi's niece, Nancy, in 1933, and because of Nancy's popularity, the strip was renamed for her in 1938. The income from the strip allowed Bushmiller to live an idyllic suburban life. Paul Karasik and Mark Newgarden write that Bushmiller and his wife, Abby, "were best friends as well as partners [who] enjoyed a marriage that worked for over half a century."[19] The Bushmillers moved from the Bronx to the suburbs of Stamford, Connecticut, in 1951. Karasik and Newgarden describe the Stamford house as follows: "[It was] large and comfortable and decorated with the work of contemporary American illustrators. . . . The rambling grounds offered ample foliage and wildlife. . . . A small grouping of rounded white rocks cropped out from the closely trimmed world outside his studio window."[20] Here, and in the studio he kept in New York, Bushmiller dedicated his life to creating *Nancy* until his death in 1982.

The pictures of Bushmiller and his colleagues that appear throughout Karasik and Newgarden's book universally show groups of white men. In the picture of the "Art Department of the 'Sunday World'" on page 32, one can see twelve formally dressed white men at their drawing boards. Karasik and Newgarden cite Leo Kober, a Sunday *World Magazine* illustrator, describing the workplace environment of the art department: "Art enchained into two columns and three columns, veloxes and silverprints, comics, pretty girls and cartoons . . . done by men devoted to a great and wonderful passion."[21] Karasik and Newgarden quote a Bushmiller neighbor who said that Bushmiller's wife, Abby, "was the ideal cartoonist's wife, attuned to the rhythm of and heartbeat of his work . . . but she also knew when to give him space."[22] Another Bushmiller colleague notes that Bushmiller "never had children. . . . I've been thinking about cartoonists, and I know there are a few exceptions to this . . . but they had either very, very small families—or no families. It was almost a characteristic of the business. Either the woman becomes part of the operation or it falls apart."[23] Here, we are firmly in the mythos of the singular, white male genius, working hard in his study, insulated from the everyday cares of the world. Women serve as "pretty girls" in the office or as wives who run the household so the creator can focus wholly on his craft.

This conception of "men devoted to a great and wonderful passion" supported by an "ideal wife" can be applied to creators from Charles Schulz to Bill Watterson. Watterson made *Calvin and Hobbes* from 1985 to 1995. He notes the singular attention he was able to give the strip during those years, thanks in part to his wife. Watterson says he "had [his] life reduced to the point where absolutely nothing unpredictable ever happened. . . . I eliminated pretty much everything from my life that wasn't the strip. My wife, Melissa, handled most everything to do with the real world, and I went at my work with a Captain Ahab–like obsession."[24] The end of *Calvin and Hobbes* can stand in for the end of a whole way of life that supported the creation of daily comic strips for white male creators. Watterson said that because of his success, "I felt indebted, like I owed the universe a lot. Having this rare opportunity was such a gift."[25] Bushmiller's working life can be thought of as this sort of gift as well. He centered his whole life around the production of *Nancy*. Very specific socioeconomic circumstances, including everything from the system of apprenticeship at New York newspapers in the 1930s to the understanding of marriage in the mid–twentieth century to the growth of the suburbs outside New York City, allowed him to focus on creating *Nancy*. Few comic creators today receive such a gift.

When the search began for a new *Nancy* creator in the mid-2010s, Andrews McMeel editor Shena Wolf said they "weren't only looking at people who had a track record in syndication."[26] Jaimes had been posting webcomics online for ten years. Some of those comics were published on GoComics, but she did not have a long history as a syndicated cartoonist. As she put it, "I've been making comics in one form or another for . . . ten years. Because, basically, as soon as I got on the internet, I just started putting things online." But she was not thinking of these webcomics as the start of a career. She did not post comics consistently: "I mean, it might be like one thing a year. Not regularly, but for that long." The interviewer asked Jaimes, "When did it start to become an obsession where you started doing it pretty regularly?" She answered, "I don't know, maybe never. I mean, doing *Nancy* is the most regular I've ever been with comics."[27] When Andrews McMeel Syndication announced the reboot of *Nancy* on April 9, 2018, they told readers little about Jaimes's life. The press release simply says, "In addition to comics, Jaimes enjoys jogging, video games and playing piano."[28] Jaimes has even worn a disguise for her rare in-person interviews, and her voice has been mechanically altered in audio interviews. Even though Jaimes's alter ego had been creating webcomics for ten years, her biography was presented as being of little importance. Whatever Jaimes's circumstances are, they are clearly not those of Bushmiller. She does not have the luxury, or perhaps the desire, to make *Nancy* her life's work. Jaimes's world and Bushmiller's world are radically different. This difference must play out in some ways in their respective *Nancy* comics. The material conditions of everyday life surrounding each creator strongly affect the comics that each has produced and the way that those comics have been received by their readers.

When she applied for the *Nancy* job, Jaimes thought of it as almost a joke. (It is important to note here that "Olivia Jaimes" is a pseudonym; while her "true" identity as the creator of a well-known webcomic is an open secret, I have no intention of discussing her "real" identity.) When an editor asked her to submit some sample strips, Jaimes said, "And I was like, 'Hahahaha, no way.' Not that I wouldn't want it—it just seemed fake. And then I'm drawing the comics to submit for the test to be like, 'Here's a couple weeks.' . . . I was like, 'Hahaha, what a funny joke this is.'"[29] The idea of making a daily syndicated comic strip "seemed fake," as if such jobs do not exist in the twenty-first century or as if a relatively unknown creator couldn't be hired to create a famous legacy comic. Once she got the job, Jaimes had no thoughts that she was embarking on a lifelong career dedicated to *Nancy*. In an interview with Jaimes, Michael Cavna reports that she "hasn't given up her day job outside of comics."[30] Jaimes says, "I'd actually recommend people think very critically about it before making a go at a career in comics."[31] Daily comic strips reach far fewer readers than they did in the past. And comic creators, even those taking on legacy strips, must work to supplement their income through merchandise and book sales, or they must have another source of income.

In the two years since its debut, Jaimes's *Nancy* has become a hit both online and in print. Web traffic for *Nancy* on GoComics, where the strip is published online, has increased 400 percent between 2018 and 2019; fans regularly engage in debate in the comments section on GoComics and in multiple Facebook groups. *Nancy*'s print-based circulation has doubled to nearly 140 newspapers since Jaimes took over.[32] A hardcover book collecting the first year of the strip was published in November 2019. While all of these things make *Nancy* a successful strip in the early twenty-first century, the numbers pale in comparison to twentieth-century syndicated daily comics, where successful comic strips regularly appeared in well over a thousand daily newspapers. It is unlikely that a comic creator working today will still be writing the same strip in twenty or thirty years. Like many jobs in the twenty-first century, the work life of comic strip creators has become precarious. Even for those creators who are picked up by a syndicate, diminished readership means that the job today can seem more like a precarious gig. Sarah Andersen, creator of *Sarah's Scribbles*, a webcomic that has been syndicated by Andrews McMeel, said in a 2015 interview, "Cartooning has changed a lot, and the way we get paid has too. You can't just get syndicated and have that be your job, unfortunately."[33] Andersen says that creators must make income from freelancing, crowdfunding sites like Patreon, merchandise sales, advertisements, and commissions. In his 2020 book, *Webcomics*, Sean Kleefeld writes of the economic difficulties faced by webcomic creators. He writes that they "might have some advertising on the site, use one crowdfunding platform as a sort of ongoing exclusive subscription, use another to fund having books printed, sell POD T-shirts and mouse pads, and occasionally do custom illustrations on commission."[34] Kleefeld emphasizes that webcomic creators who want to make doing comics their primary source of income might have to do all these things "to bring in enough . . . to make a living."[35] As an occupation, then, webcomic creators always have to be working to earn as much as they can from multiple revenue sources. Most of these income sources are unpredictable, so creators cannot count on a specific amount of income from any one reliable income stream.

Andrew Ross's 2009 book, *Nice Work If You Can Get It: Life and Labor in Precarious Times*, analyzes how and why multiple fields of labor, from low-wage service jobs to high-earning creative jobs, have become unstable in the twenty-first century. He writes, "No one, not even those in the traditional professions, can any longer expect a fixed pattern of employment in the course of their lifetime, and they are under more and more pressure to anticipate, and prepare for, a future in which they still will be able to compete in a changing marketplace."[36] The "changing marketplace" that Ross mentions demands worker flexibility.

The work life that Olivia Jaimes describes differs radically from what we know of the work lives of most twentieth-century comic strip creators. These changes have broad ramifications for the relationship between creators and readers, for the actual content of strips, for the ways strips get read, and for how strips comment on contemporary culture. The old model, exemplified by Bushmiller and which I roughly date from the 1930s to the 1990s, entailed earning a good wage and a secure career working for a syndicate and having a lifestyle that allowed one to focus wholly on comic creation. The new model of comic creation, which started when comic strips began running online in the late 1990s and early 2000s, entails communicating with fans; having more than one income source; self-publishing on the web; and hustling for income through merchandise sales, commissions, subscriptions, and freelance work. Stephen Pastis's *Pearls before Swine* can serve as a dividing line between the old print syndicate model and the new flexible publication model. Sean Kleefeld notes that Pastis's comic was one of the first times a syndicate experimented with web publication, "as his strip was essentially launched as a webcomic by his syndicate as a test to see readers' reactions before they tried selling it to newspapers."[37] Pastis's comic was published on comics.com beginning in November 2000, during which time Pastis was "watching the traffic numbers and getting direct and immediate feedback from readers."[38] After more than a year of online publication, Pastis's strip was sold to newspapers. From this point on, the number of newspapers that ran a strip, instead of being the main way to determine a comic strip's popularity, became just one data point among many. More granular data—such as online comments on individual strips and free and premium subscription numbers—gave syndicates more information about how readers interacted with comic strips.

Flexible Materialism

Ernesto Priego's 2013 essay, "On Cultural Materialism, Comics and Digital Media," serves as a call for a "cultural materialist" approach to comics, "to illuminate what comics are or are capable of being" in our digital age.[39] Priego defines his area of interest as "the still-transitional stage in which comics co-exist in different platforms and how new ways of creating, publishing and therefore reading are being put to test."[40] Priego wants to interrogate how the medium of comics (paper and digital screens) affects what comics are and how comics are read, and he asks how the materiality of a comic affects its creation, content, and reception. Many comic scholars have discussed the importance of the material form in which a reader consumes comics. Charles Hatfield, in his *Alternative Comics*, writes about "the dimensions of comics as material objects" concisely defined as "not only the design or layout of the page but also the physical makeup of the text, including its size, shape, binding, paper, and printing."[41] The physicality of the text is an integral part of "meaning-making," and according to Hatfield "many comics make it impossible to distinguish between text per se and secondary aspects such as design and the physical package" in communicating meaning and involving readers in interpretation.[42] Likewise, in her 2020 book, *Comics and the Body*, Eszter Szép argues that the physicality of a comic can strongly affect how it is read: "Reading any comics is an encounter with the dimension, weight, materials, fragility, and all the physical characteristics of the published object or of the device on which the comic is read in a given environment."[43]

This call for a material study of comics has been taken up by Kashtan in *Between Pen and Pixel*. Kashtan defines materiality "as the way in which the physical, technological, and sensuous components of a media artifact help to shape the reader's reception of that media artifact."[44] For Kashtan, comics demand that attention be paid to this "material rhetoric," to the ways that physical form influences how readers "comprehend" meaning.[45] Kashtan pays detailed attention to comics that work best in different media, like print comics that use nonstandard-size pages and nonlinear reading structures that do not easily translate to digital media, as well as digital comics that use point-and-click, scrolling, hypertext, and touch-screen technologies that cannot easily be translated to the page. For the purpose of this study of *Nancy*, though, I am most interested in what Kashtan calls "flexible" comics that can be read in multiple formats, as I discuss above.

Henry Jenkins's 2019 book, *Comics and Stuff*, takes materialism in a slightly different and broader direction. He writes, "I explore the relationship between comics and material culture— what makes comics an important medium for reflecting upon people's relationships with stuff?"[46] Jenkins shares other materialist critics' interest in the rhetorical modes of comics, but he also focuses on the objects that make up the content of graphic novels. He focuses on works that center collectors of arcane things and accumulators of everyday objects, because such works pay close attention to the meaning of "stuff": "This collector mentality leads to a particular emphasis on the roles that seemingly mundane or ordinary objects play in our everyday lives—their hidden meaning and unsuspected value."[47] The extraordinarily close attention that a collector might pay to old comics, vinyl records, or toys, for example, shows readers how we make meaning from such objects. Jenkins makes the salient point that objects in comics are intentional: "Because comics take place in a completely fabricated world, everything is there by design. Yet why place so many objects within view if we are intended to read past them?"[48] For Jenkins, "stuff" has representational value—it tells us about the meanings that characters attach to things: "Comics are stuff; comics tell stories about stuff; and they display stuff."[49] Comics themselves are material objects, and they focus on material things, which readers should interpret to find meaning in what characters value and how characters see the world. Jenkins's focus on "stuff" is a focus on the multiple levels of materiality that comics are immersed in.

Eszter Szép offers a different take on materiality, in *Comics and the Body*. Rather than focusing on how materiality might reveal a character's state of mind, Szép focuses on the embodied "dialogue" that takes place between "drawers" and readers. Szép's use of "drawers" instead of the more common "artist," "writer," or "creator" brings attention to the "drawn line" that is fundamental to comics and to the "the trace of the drawer's hand" in their work.[50] For Szép the act of reading comics is always embodied: "Engagement with comics takes place, on the one hand, by the involvement of the drawer's and reader's bodies, and on the other hand, by interacting with the materiality of the actual comics that is mediating the interaction"; as the "drawer, reader, and object (the actual comic)" interact, a kind of "transformative dialogue" takes place through the vulnerable connection of bodies.[51] It is important to note that Szép focuses on nonfiction comics because they "claim that they have a special connection to reality" based "on the person of the author, who is the key to the credibility of the work."[52] The material connections created by fiction comics do not share this grounding in claims of truth and authenticity. Nonetheless, Szép's focus on bodily interaction between drawers and readers can be broadly applied to all acts of reading comics. In a similar way, Ian Hague's *Comics and the Senses* argues for a material reading practice grounded in the body. Hague focuses on the sensory aspects of reading and creating. He argues that "the physicality of comics, their embodiment, is a crucial element of what they are and what they can be; how they do work, and how they could work."[53] For Hague every act of reading is different because of the "multiplicity of elements" involved in a reader's interaction with a comic. Hague notes that different aspects, from a reader's sensory experience at the time of reading to the actual text itself, may be more or less involved in any one reading. Most importantly, he claims that "materiality is not on/off in terms of its significance, it is always on."[54] In my focus on materiality, I strongly agree with Hague here. Materiality is *always on* in both a temporal and spatial sense. Every act of creating and reading a comic strip happens in a specific time and place that strongly affects both creation and interpretation. While readers can emphasize certain aspects of the context of reading, we do not have a choice to turn off the material conditions and escape into an objective world of universal meaning. Materiality can never be turned off.

For my reading of comics in general and *Nancy* in particular, I want to offer a more expansive take on materialism that I call "flexible materialism." Flexible materialism does not dispute the claims of any of the scholars of materiality I have discussed already; rather, it combines and amplifies these claims. I want to bring together Priego's focus on cultural materialism, Kashtan's focus on rhetorical materiality, Jenkins's focus on representational materiality, and Szép's and Hague's focus on bodily materiality.[55] To these, I want to add insights from the fields of new materialism and object-oriented ontology, without fully subscribing to either (in large part because neither of those fields focuses on comics). Flexible materialism claims that the limits of materialism can never be marked; another aspect of materiality can always be added to the study of a comic. Flexible materialism takes account of the always-on materiality of comic strips in their print and digital forms. It likewise pays close attention to the material objects that appear in the diegetic space of the strip—that is, in the world represented within the panels, such as cell phones, computers, desks, windows, doors, trees, bushes, rocks, animals, and people. The narrative of a comic like *Nancy* depends just as much on inanimate objects as it does on its characters. It is as difficult today to imagine the strip without Sluggo as it is without Nancy's phone. Importantly, flexible materiality extends beyond the diegetic space of the comic strip, to the comments section on the strip's GoComics page, to Facebook groups about *Nancy*, to the material objects of *Nancy* fandom such as T-shirts and pins, to the pseudonymous construction of Olivia Jaimes through print interviews, public disguises, and voice-modulated YouTube videos, to the readers who engage with the strip in multiple ways. When I refer to *Nancy* as a flexible comic strip or to Jaimes as a flexible creator, I mean that both strip and creator adapt to all of these aspects of materiality: to being online and in print, to blurring the lines between work and life, to questioning the space between the diegetic and extradiegetic. Flexible creators make these adaptations visible on the page and in the world; they work to show readers the materiality that underlies their comics. Also, as individual creators take on all the financial risk of comic creation, they must constantly respond to changing circumstances. As Megan Brown reminds us in "Survival at Work: Flexibility and Adaptability in American Corporate Culture," "flexibility itself may carry a steep price: the flexible worker must remain flexible *at all times*, and must constantly train him/herself in order to become even more flexible."[56] If they are not flexible, comic creators might lose readers' attention. It can be difficult to draw a line where work ends—creators must constantly ask themselves how much time should be dedicated not just to writing and drawing but also to interacting with readers across multiple platforms.

What I am calling "flexible materialism" bears some resemblance to the kind of "cultural materialism" that Priego, following Raymond Williams, defines as "a complex and fluid series of interconnected dialectic relationships between people, ideas and physical objects in sets of specific spatiotemporal conditions of geographical, political, economic, technological and ideological order."[57] Cultural materialism understands art through its material instantiations and as an expression of specific ideological assumptions, as it focuses on "questions of causality and agency."[58] In addition to these questions, I add the question of how materiality relates to form. Many comic strips can move between print and digital, but *Nancy* (and certainly others) takes this further. In what follows, I will argue that form is always materially situated to the point that form becomes a subset of flexible materiality. Form emerges from the material conditions of its time and cannot be separated from those conditions. Contemporary flexible comics like *Nancy* show a self-reflexive awareness of their own material conditions. Jaimes's new *Nancy* moves within the legacy of Ernie Bushmiller's long-running comic, yet it also takes into account appropriations of Bushmiller's work, contemporary fandom, feminism, racial representation, social media, and the history of comics. In her strip, Jaimes finds ways to graphically represent the spaces where all these things interact, by using multiple strategies to render visible what might otherwise go unseen.

I want to note here that comic strips self-reflexively taking account of their material conditions is not new; it is in fact as old as comics themselves. Rather, what is new for contemporary flexible comics is the material contexts that shape them. Ian Gordon, a historian of comics, has shown that the growing popularity of newspaper comics in the later nineteenth and early twentieth century profoundly shaped their formal elements. Gordon argues that comic creators gave their characters unique personalities by creating what we now take for granted as basic components of comic strips. He writes, "Artists created mechanisms basic to the comic strip as means of embellishing their characters. Devices such as panels and word balloons worked to elaborate and extend these characters by placing them in narratives and supplying them with voices."[59] Breaking comics up into panels and normalizing their way of speaking through word balloons helped artists to give their characters life, to make them stand apart from other characters. In turn, these unique characters led to new means of creation and production, as "characters laid the basis for widespread distribution of comic strips and development of the formal properties of the art form that later proved useful for advertising."[60] The formal properties of comics have always worked hand in hand with the material conditions of their production. The formal tools that allowed creators to give their characters personalities developed alongside the material practices of the newspaper and advertising industries of their day. Likewise, flexible twenty-first-century comics like *Nancy* must develop formal elements that connect to the material practices of the digital and print comic industry of today.

As I consider *Nancy* as a twenty-first-century flexible comic, I read it as having what the object-oriented ontologist Graham Harman calls a "flat ontology." Ontology can be understood as the study of being or even the study of reality itself. Most ontologists argue that human thought and perception lie at the center of being (think of Descartes's "Cogito, Ergo Sum"); rejecting the human as the seat of being, flat ontology "initially treats all objects in the same way, rather than assuming in advance that different types of objects require completely different ontologies."[61] In flat ontology, a rock has the same kind of being as a person, a comic dog exists on the same plane as a reader, a fictional character shares being with a real person. Flat ontology might not sound immediately applicable to comics, but a few comic scholars have begun to use some of the tenets of object-oriented ontology. Sebastian Bartosch's

"Understanding Comics' Mediality as an Actor-Network" uses Bruno Latour's actor-network theory to argue that "being actors themselves, the comics rest on the same level as the network of mediality they are part of."[62] Neither form nor content precedes the other in this kind of analysis. Likewise, what counts as an actor worthy of study is expansive: "Agencies are distributed between human and non-human entities, organic and inorganic matter, and where objects, bodies, and subjectivities emerge as relational effects."[63] Bartosch uses the comics of Brian Fies and Dylan Horrocks as the agents of his study, but his discussion can apply to the subject of this book. Nancy's subjectivity emerges through the act of reading, but so does the reader's. Nancy writes a blog within the world of the strip. This shapes her personality, but it also shapes the content and the meaning of the comic for digital readers.[64]

My approach also bears similarities to what has become known as "new materialism." In their collection, *New Materialisms: Ontology, Agency, and Politics*, Diana Coole and Samantha Frost make what they call a bold claim: "Foregrounding material factors and reconfiguring our very understanding of matter are prerequisites for any plausible account of coexistence and its conditions in the twenty-first century."[65] The word "coexistence" does a lot of work for Coole and Frost here. New materialism understands all existence to be a form of coexistence. No one thing can be understood on its own. Everything bears a material connection to something else. New materialism can help locate a space where the materiality *of* and *in* a comic strip such as *Nancy* points to new ways of living in the twenty-first century. This claim might sound grandiose, but it is actually quite mundane. When Coole and Frost call for readers "to recognize that phenomena are caught in a multitude of interlocking systems and forces and to consider anew the location and nature of capacities for agency," they are focused on aspects of everyday life.[66] To cite one of their examples, "Whether it is pacing the heartbeat, dispensing medication, catching the news on a podcast, elaborating an internet-based community, finding directions via the web or GPS, or sending family love via wireless communications, digital technologies have become a part of our lives and of who we are."[67] Importantly, new materialism does not prejudge these mundane relationships—it is neither technophobic nor technoutopian. In the example I cite, and elsewhere, the authors are simply technorealistic. These are the things we do every day, and these things have become intimate parts of our subjectivity. This technorealism also points to why I think new materialism is a useful way of thinking about hybrid comics like *Nancy*. Digital technology plays a large role in the strip, but it is seen neither as a negative influence on children nor as a means of ultimate freedom. It is just one more thing that Nancy and her friends engage with and through every day, just as readers engage *Nancy* through multiple technologies.

In fact, most versions of materialism, almost by definition, focus on mundane experience, going back to Karl Marx himself. As Marx wrote in his *German Ideology*, "As individuals express their life, so they are. What they are, therefore, coincides with their production, both with what they produce and with how they produce. The nature of individuals thus depends on the material conditions determining their production."[68] From the perspective of flexible materialism, the working life of a creator must affect their creation. A few more points of contrast between Bushmiller and Jaimes can show how.

As I discuss above, Bushmiller was able to cultivate a life that allowed him to focus fully on his comic strip. His "ideal" wife and his house in the suburbs gave him the seclusion he craved. He could isolate himself at his drawing board in his office and cut off the outside world. In *Nancy* he strove to avoid any commentary on the wider world. Karasik and Newgarden quote Bushmiller as saying, "I have never gotten an idea from real life."[69] Alone at his drawing board, he focused purely on humor, in search of what he called "the Perfect Gag." He once wrote, "Mine is a lonely business—I often sit at my drawing board and . . . talk to myself."[70] His niece said of him, "He was always stashed in his room, drawing. . . . He put his love into the cartoon."[71] Bushmiller attempted to cut himself off from the outside world in the service of his work. It is, of course, truly impossible to remove oneself from the social, political, and economic contexts of everyday life. What is important here is to note that Bushmiller idealized this type of isolation.[72] Bushmiller had little interaction with his fans, mostly through rare public appearances and slow correspondence through mailed letters.

What Jaimes has revealed of her working life seems much more chaotic. She describes how she uses the Notes app on her phone to jot down ideas for *Nancy* strips. She says that the "vast majority" of cartoonists she knows work in a similar way, jotting down ideas as they occur and using these ideas to generate strips. In an interview, Jaimes shared some of her notes, including one that said, "Coupon good for one floor clean of macaroni card." This brief note led directly to a strip: "And that's one that came out, I think, sometime in the last month, where Nancy's doing something nice for Aunt Fritzi and she makes her a macaroni card coupon, with a coupon just to clean the floor when all the macaroni falls off."[73] The strip with the macaroni coupon was published on October 6, 2018. Jaimes goes on to say that her ideas list often gets mixed with her to-do list. As she continues looking at her notes during the interview, she says, "And then, underneath, I also have my to-do list of things to buy. It says 'gloves.' . . . And I haven't even bought gloves yet, so it's really good that I remember. It's getting cold."[74] In this brief discussion, Jaimes deromanticizes the ideal of a creator in an isolated room wholly focused on their work. A Notes app on a phone is portable and ready-to-hand at all times. Ideas can be generated anywhere, at any time. Likewise, by noting how her lists combine strip ideas and reminders to do tasks, Jaimes blurs the line between her work and her life in a humorous way, even using the forum of an interview (which is a kind of work) to remind herself to buy gloves. In short, Jaimes comes across as relatable to a contemporary audience in this anecdote, as she recalls typing and forgetting notes, remembering things at the wrong time, and having her work and life intersect. Considering the overlap between work and life, contemporary comic creators are expected to have a certain degree of engagement with fans through social media, newsletters, comic conventions, and even personalized merchandise sales. In short, both creator and creation must be not only flexible but also relatable.

Becoming #Relatable

A flexible comic can be read in both print and digital formats; its creator thus has to account for two audiences and make a connection with both print and digital readers. The task of creating a relationship with readers can be especially difficult in a legacy comic like *Nancy*. Briefly defined, a legacy comic is a strip that continues after its original creator dies, retires, or quits. Legacy comic strips come with their own histories of drawing style, character relationships, types of humor, and areas of interest. Its creator must relate to readers who have a long familiarity with a strip, who are more likely to read it in a newspaper, *and* to readers who might have just discovered the strip online. In this section, I want to show how a flexible comic creator needs to fashion a relatable persona, generate relatable representations, and produce relatable humor, all for a diverse audience.

Becoming relatable entails a lot of work for a creator, placing a difficult question at the heart of their work: Relatable to whom? A beginning answer to this question is simply "relatable to somebody." Webcomic creators sometimes relate to a narrow, specific audience. Kleefeld writes that "webcomics are, by and large, fairly niche in their targeting and difficult to speak to significantly sized audiences."[75] As webcomics can be published without traditional gatekeepers (editors and publishers), a creator can post comics "with little concern about whether there is a sufficient audience for the material."[76] A syndicated flexible comic creator has to think about a wider audience, so the relatable "somebody" can be much harder to define. Relatability might best be understood as an open-ended relationship. Focusing on relatability makes specific connections visible. Jaimes's *Nancy* can be read as relatable to millennials, to girls and young women, to people who spend a lot of time online, and to people who enjoy metahumor. While these characteristics might make a connection between the strip and its readers, this list can never be complete. Likewise, Jaimes's *Nancy* might not be relatable to older fans of Bushmiller's *Nancy* who see themselves as guardians of certain formalist and aesthetic values. But there is obviously no way to make a list of who Jaimes's *Nancy* is and is not relatable to. Rather, focusing on questions of relatability serves to illustrate the nonuniversality of *Nancy* or any comic strip.

Claims of universality often serve as attempts to set cultural and aesthetic norms. Universalizing claims of whiteness as the cultural and aesthetic norm in America are a primary example of how such claims work. Critics have noted how such universalizing claims have been long present in American culture, from nineteenth-century literature to contemporary superhero stories. Toni Morrison has written about how early American literature imagined a common desire for "the American Dream" by creating "a whole tradition of 'universal' yearning" for freedom. Yet, Morrison writes, this desire was framed by white male writers who created Black characters only as a means of self-reflection. Morrison writes that, in the works of early American white male writers, "the appearance of Africanist characters or narrative or idiom in a work could never be *about* anything other than the 'normal,' unracialized illusory white world that provided the fictional backdrop."[77] One of Morrison's goals is to show that such claims of universal desire are always illusory. And while it might seem like a long leap from early American literature to superhero narratives, Sean Guynes and Martin Lund argue that superhero stories traffic in a similar understanding of whiteness as universal. They write that "the superhero genre has historically been bound up with the logic of mass-market appeal that sees the majority of its audience as racially unmarked, and therefore white. In other words, superhero comics creators overwhelmingly, even if not consciously, assume white faces, bodies, and experiences to be the universal standards of American life."[78] Thinking of cultural works as relatable to a specific "somebody" and not a universal "everybody" can work against such universalizing claims.

In other words, relatability rejects the universal and favors the situational. Feminist science studies scholar Donna Haraway coined the term "situated knowledges" in 1988 against the idea that scientific understanding could ever be a product of "universal rationality."[79] For Haraway, knowledge cannot "pretend . . . to be from everywhere and so nowhere, to be free from interpretation, from being represented, to be fully self-contained or fully formalizable."[80] Rather, for Haraway, all knowledge comes from an embodied somewhere, from a specific ground. More recently, Haraway has emphasized that the situational is always relational. Further, she understands that the category of relational is expansive and open-ended. She has recently written that other words for "situated knowledges" might be "materialism, evolution, ecology . . . history . . . complete with the contaminations and infections conjured by each of these terms."[81] Relatability cannot be contained by any one or several terms. To be relatable is to forge material connections and to reject universal understanding. Relatability can be said to be inescapable. A reader might or might not relate to *Nancy* as a computer-literate, middle-class teenage girl or as a computer-averse, middle-aged, formalist-critic man. Relationality is always happening whether we want to acknowledge it or not.

Contemporary flexible comic strips like Jaimes's *Nancy* illustrate the centrality of relatability to their success. A creator whose work appears online has to create a persona to interact with readers, as the success of so many webcomics depends financially on the relationship between creator and reader. I will discuss webcomics more in chapter 1, but for now it suffices to say that a webcomic is a comic published online, usually without the backing of an editor or a syndicate, which of course means that most webcomic creators are unpaid. Hilary Chute compares webcomics to both punk rock and underground comics, as they are "a platform that similarly aims for direct, uncensored, immediate communication."[82] Critics like Chute and Scott McCloud celebrate the freedom of web publication, with McCloud championing the "infinite canvas" that publishing online allows.[83] Of course, if anyone can publish a webcomic, then a lot of people will publish webcomics, which in turn means that most webcomics will not find even a tiny audience, let alone reach a point where they can make money. Not everyone publishing a webcomic necessarily wants to make a career in comics. Those who do have to work hard to get their work noticed. As Kleefeld writes in *Webcomics*, "With webcomics, even finding an audience for the webcomic itself does not mean that a creator has found an audience of people willing to spend money on whatever they might have to sell."[84] Creators must engage fans in multiple ways, on multiple social media platforms, through online shops, in email newsletters, through subscription-based spaces like Patreon, and even in person at comic conventions. Malcolm Harris, in *Kids These Days: Human Capital and the Making of Millennials*, writes that "building a brand is no longer the purview of slick besuited experts; it's the individual responsibility of every voice that wants to make it."[85] Webcomic creators have to build themselves as a brand to make an income from their work.

Webcomic creators want their comics to be relatable to specific audiences. Of course, all comics to a certain degree want to be relatable, to have readers identify with characters' thoughts, actions, and motivations. But for comics published primarily online, relatability (often stylized as "#relatable") can be thought of as a kind of currency. In an interview, Jaimes discusses the complexities of #relatable in webcomics and how she addresses this complexity in her first *Nancy* strip. She notes that #relatable can be used as a positive or negative term: "There's this thing in webcomics: #relatable. And #relatable can be used as a slur. To be like, 'Uh, your comic is pandering to people.'"[86] There's a fine line between being truly #relatable and pandering, and that line can be difficult to demarcate, as it often depends on individual readers and communities. One can find multitudes of webcomics on the subreddit r/comics that are labeled #pandering and a similar number labeled #relatable. Comics that are seen as #pandering are characterized as trying too hard to form a connection with an audience. In the early 2010s, Matt Inman's popular webcomic *The Oatmeal* became a flash point for defining pandering when it was revealed that he had previously worked in the field of search engine optimization. Certain readers accused Inman of using the tools of online marketing to create a broad audience for his comic. Max Read's disparaging critique of *The Oatmeal* defines what makes a comic pandering: "The Oatmeal doesn't feel like something from its creator's brain, marked by its creator's obsessions, driven by its creator's passions, the way even the worst newspaper strips do. It feels like something written by a committee. Or an algorithm."[87] Comics that pander get dismissed as engineered to find readers, while #relatable comics form connections with readers through establishing characters' idiosyncrasies over the course of the comics' development. Regardless of the line between #pandering and #relatable, Jaimes asserts that she wants Nancy to be #relatable. She says, "I think it's great to be relatable, and I don't want people to use relatable as an insult. I feel like Nancy is #relatable."[88] Before doing a reading of Jaimes's first *Nancy* strip, which instantly portrays Nancy as #relatable, I want to offer a bit of historical context regarding the meaning of "relatable" and then discuss the gendered nature of online relatability.

Jaimes notes a tension in how #relatable gets understood— either as pandering or as a positive means of connection—that speaks to the broader origins of the word's use in popular culture. In her 2014 *New Yorker* essay, "The Scourge of Relatability," Rebecca Mead traces contemporary usage of the word to the 1990s. She argues that relatability "first was popularized by the television industry" and specifically by daytime talk shows. Mead cites Rosie O'Donnell's 1996 claim about connecting to her audience—"It's the stories about living your life that makes you relatable to your audience"—as a formative moment in how "relatable" has come to be understood.[89] For Mead, the understanding of "relatable" as a way "to describe a character or a situation in which an ordinary person might see himself reflected" points to a societal failure in how we interact with aesthetic works, be they literature, television shows, or movies. To focus on how readers or viewers see themselves reflected in a work "serves like a selfie: a flattering confirmation of an individual's solipsism." In this configuration, relatability works as a passive discovery of a reader's or viewer's self in the work. This passivity, embodied in the pleasure of self-affirmation, precludes what Mead sees as the more important work of readership and viewership that would entail "the active exercise of imagination or the effortful summoning of empathy."[90] A relatable work, then, is one that is easy to experience, a work in which one sees oneself and thus has no desire to move outside this limited frame of reflection. To move beyond self-reflection would require active reading that tries to understand otherness as something different from the self. For Mead, then, "relatable" is a "scourge," because it is nothing but pandering.

While Mead dismisses relatability as too simple a way to engage a text, she notes that the concept has roots in the Freudian concept of identification, the "means whereby an individual develops his or her personality through idealizing and imitating a parent or other figure."[91] This psychoanalytic understanding of identification became hugely influential in literary criticism in the 1970s, in part because it provided a way to think about "the pleasures of reading" that come about in identifying with a character. Reader-response theory found its ground in this kind of interpretation. Jane Tompkins, one of the critics most identified with this methodology, writes that reader-response theory "uses the idea of the reader as a means of producing a new kind of textual analysis, and it suggests that literary criticism be seen as part of larger, more fundamental processes such as *the forming of an identity*."[92] That is, identification with elements of a text came to be seen as a legitimate means of understanding and interpreting literary works. A reader's connection to and ways of reacting to a work became, according to Tompkins, "a legitimate basis for literary interpretation."[93] Reader identification with aspects of a work has become commonplace since Tompkins wrote these words more than forty years ago. Identity-based theory and criticism informs a wide range of methodologies, from cognitive media theory, to intersectionality, to what Laura M. Jiménez has called "social media and critical race literary criticism."[94] Cognitive media theory centers a viewer's connection to a work, with "a general focus on the mental activity of viewers as the central (but not the only) object of inquiry."[95] Intersectional approaches examine the connections between individual identities and structural power to examine "how power shifts in relation to people's identities in order to make visible often invisible marginalized communities."[96] Social media and critical race literary criticism established the #OwnVoices movement in 2015. Crisp and colleagues write that "the #OwnVoices hashtag was created on Twitter by Corinne Duyvis, an author of young adult literature, to refer to 'kidlit about diverse characters written by authors from that same diverse group.'"[97] #OwnVoices was meant as a shorthand way "to recommend books by authors who openly shared the diverse identity of their main characters."[98]

#OwnVoices strongly linked an author's identity to their characters and thus can serve as a case study for thinking about the benefits and costs of identity-based criticism. Maria V. Acevedo-Aquino and colleagues argue that "#OwnVoices books have an added richness because the author shares an identity with the character, with the deepest understanding of the intricacies, the joys, the difficulties, the pride, the frustration, and every other possible facet of that particular life—because the author has actually lived it."[99] Critics have noted that #OwnVoices books such as "Angie Thomas' *The Hate U Give*, Celeste Ng's *Everything I Never Told You*, [and Corrine] Duyvis' . . . *On the Edge of Gone* have all earned well-deserved acclaim."[100] At the same time, the use of #OwnVoices can place serious burdens on authors who do not wish to publicly reveal an aspect of their identity. S. E. Smith notes that "there's increasing pressure for authors to divulge personal information, even if it endangers them or feels too intimate."[101] Some authors may fear identity-based discrimination if they reveal aspects of their mental health. Others worry about the dangers of physical violence, as Smith notes that "people with intellectual disabilities experience higher rates of physical and sexual assault [and] demanding details about their lives can put them at risk."[102] #OwnVoices can also put pressure on writers to reveal things they would rather keep private. Leigh Bardugo "felt pressured to disclose her history as a survivor of sexual assault prior to the publication of her 2019 adult novel *Ninth House*" and said, "I don't believe that I should have to put that on display to justify writing a novel. . . . I'm disturbed by the performances we require of women authors."[103] The burden of showing that one can be #relatable often falls on women authors and creators.

When the *Nancy* reboot was announced in 2018, the press release said little about Jaimes's identity, but it did note that *Nancy* would be written and drawn by a woman for the first time: "We're going on almost 100 years of a man writing for *Nancy* and we loved the idea that Olivia had this delicious blend of love for the old Bushmiller work and a 21st century female perspective that would bring new life to this iconic character."[104] While it would be impossible to fully define every aspect of "a 21st century female perspective," I want to pay attention to the connection between this gendered identity and relatability.

In a recent Slate essay, "The Awful Emptiness of 'Relatable,'" Rebecca Onion laments the use of the term "relatable" by students in college and university classrooms. For her, when students describe a literary character or historical figure as more or less relatable, discussion and possible insight get shortchanged. Onion writes, "The quest for the 'relatable' circumscribes the expansion of empathy that you can gain through exposure to new things. When the word 'relatable' really means 'relevant to me,' as it often does in the classroom, anything outside the purview of 'relatability' looks like it's not worth examining."[105] Onion's argument here seems almost commonsensical. Her disdain for the "relatable" in the classroom is only the first part of her argument, though. Out of annoyance and curiosity, Onion goes online to research the contemporary use of "relatable" and finds something interesting: the "cottage industry" of "relatable content" on Tumblr and Twitter. She discovers that most of the memes she finds "seem to come from a female point of view. Tweets feature cute male celebrities, nostalgic roundups of favorite Disney characters, and jokes about menstrual cycles and body image. . . . 'Relatable' Twitter externalizes sadness, desire, and weakness." She concludes, "Could 'relatable' Twitter and Tumblr be spaces for girls to feel better about shared experiences that would otherwise be painful? Far be it from me to deny them!"[106] Following Onion, #relatable can be read as a female-gendered term through which girls and young women make connections and share experiences. Count Nancy in this group.

In her 2019 book, *Gender and Relatability in Digital Culture: Managing Affect, Intimacy and Value*, Akane Kanai provides a thoroughly researched foundation that corroborates Rebecca Onion's thought that #relatable marks a primarily female digital space. Kanai begins her book by discussing a meme that a friend shared with her of a drunk young woman stumbling in high heels. She writes, "This post was voiced as personal, relating to its author, but also generalisable to other readers' experiences who shared a similar socio-cultural, gendered and classed position in accepting the invitation to relate to this moment"[107] From this moment, Kanai formulates a question that drives her research: "What kind of work had gone into producing this relatability?"[108] Kanai then asks questions "about the structures and politics of such relatability, and the ordering of feminine subjectivities through them as part of broader shifts in subjectivity in neoliberal culture."[109] While Kanai's research focuses on memes, what she writes can also apply to #relatable comics like *Nancy*.

Food, and its relation to body image, is perhaps one of the most common #relatable tropes. Kanai dedicates a whole section of her book to food and body management. She writes, "It is . . . unsurprising that food consumption is one of the key preoccupations managed and worked through" in certain lifestyle blogs.[110] Olivia Jaimes employs it often, and in her very first *Nancy* strip. Comic creators, of course, have long used food consumption as a staple joke. Bushmiller's gags often revolved around Nancy's desire for cake, cookies, and ice cream. *Peanuts* regularly featured characters discussing candy, and Snoopy's supper dish and dinner dance were long-running jokes. Gluttony, from Little Lulu's friend Tubby to Bob Weber's titular Moose Miller to Garfield's love of lasagna, has served as a primary trait for many characters.

Food as #relatable works differently in online comics for one key reason: a reader's ability to easily and quickly respond. Readers can like, retweet, add their own hashtags, comment, and create memes online. A #relatable food comic might go viral, or it might disappear without a trace. Jaimes notes that #relatable contains multiple components, and she uses them in her first *Nancy* comic. Jaimes notes, however, that there is a "self-hating part" of #relatable that she tries to avoid in her comics: "So, there's the camp of #relatable, which is like, 'I'm the worst person: I can't stop eating bread,' or 'I can't get out of bed,' and like, Nancy is that, but then she's also like, 'So what?' . . . The self-hating part that often comes with #relatable comics is being like, 'Ohhhh, I procrastinated, I'm the worst.' And 'Nancy' adds one more panel to that, being like, 'Who cares? I don't care. More corn bread for me.'"[111]

Jaimes writes Nancy to be #relatable in this way from her very first comic on April 9, 2018. In the first three panels, we see Nancy seated at a table on which increasing piles of food are placed, while an unnamed woman comments. The final panel shifts to a full view of the woman's head (we can no longer see Nancy at the table) as she says, "Wow, she is going *in* on that cornbread." Nancy's love of food is presented in an almost absurdist way. In the first three panels, Nancy sits at the table with the exact same posture (except for her arms being in different positions) with the exact same smile on her face. The table and chair appear in an otherwise empty room, with the contours of a floor and wall marked by a single line. Nancy's slice of pie sits on a tray in the first panel, as if it might be part of a school lunch. In the second panel, she holds the fork in her fist, like she has no idea how to use it. She appears to be pouring salt onto her slice of pie. In panel 3, she holds a stick of butter as if she is about to take a bite from it. Readers get a small glimpse of the corn bread that features in the words in panel 4. From panel to panel, the comic seems both logical and illogical. Readers can understand that time passes between panels, but they will have no idea where all this food has come from or how much time has passed. Has Nancy gathered and eaten all this food between each panel? Likewise, Nancy's facial expression tells us little about her inner state. She looks neither hungry nor satiated, and her facial expression does not change.

Nancy embraces her love of food; she rarely doubts herself and definitely does not hate herself. Nancy does not care what you think about her desire for corn bread. Jaimes returns to Nancy's fascination with food regularly. On May 10, 2018, Nancy sits in her classroom while her teacher lectures about internet research. In the final panel, we see Nancy looking at her laptop screen, which displays a picture of a sundae and the words "Top Ten Ice Cream Flavors (You need to try before your die!!!)," as Nancy says aloud, "Good thing I stick to reliable sources." On May 26, 2018, Nancy's friend Esther looks at what appears to be Nancy's Instagram page to "get a real sense of who she is as a person." The strip's final panel reveals nine square photos, each of ice cream. As I will discuss in chapter 3, Nancy's desire for cookies underlies the humor of multiple strips. Nancy loves food, and she loves to read and post about her love of food online. Before she is anything else in Jaimes's reboot, Nancy is #relatable.

Jaimes uses relatability in a way specific to webcomics, but I want to argue that this first strip, and all subsequent ones, is also flexible. It works online and in print, too, in part because Jaimes works within the conventions of newspaper comic strips that will be familiar to many readers. *Nancy* employs what comic scholar Thierry Groensteen calls, in his foundational *The System of Comics*, a "regular layout."[112] *Nancy*, like most daily newspaper comics, usually uses four square panels separated by lined gutters. Each panel follows the one before it in sequential order, left to right. The Sunday comic stacks three four-panel strips so that it can be read left to right and top to bottom. Any reader of daily comic strips knows this—such a "regular" layout seems invisible and logical. As Groensteen notes, such comics are easy to read because "the frames are more than compatible because they are identical and no doubt is introduced to the reader with regard to the order in which the panels are linked."[113] In addition, Groensteen argues that "a regular page layout . . . allows for the most simple and striking way of organizing things from the point of view of perception, and because it strengthens the bonds between predetermined locations."[114] That is, a regular page layout provides a kind of unity—readers know that each panel follows the other left to right in terms of chronological sequence and spatial organization.

Jaimes's first *Nancy* strip illustrates the ease with which a regularly laid-out strip can be read. The panels clearly work sequentially; as time passes, Nancy eats more and more food as we read from left to right. We can easily determine that the unnamed speaker is watching Nancy eat and offering commentary. We also clearly understand the spatialization of the strip. The first three panels take place in the same space, a kitchen or dining room, with the speaker in profile at the left edge of the panel in the foreground and Nancy farther back in the center of the frame. All that changes in the first three panels are the speaker's words, the objects in Nancy's hands, and the food on the table. The speaker comments, and Nancy consumes in the space between panels. The final panel shifts to a close-up of the speaker's face to emphasize the enthusiasm with which Nancy consumes corn bread, with the word "in" appearing larger than the other words for emphasis. The strip achieves a comic effect by leaving Nancy's actual eating to the imagination. We see her sitting somewhat primly at the table, but based on the narrator's words and the shift in perspective in panel 4, readers can assume but cannot see Nancy's gluttony. The act of reading that I have just described, following Groensteen's definition of "regular layout," takes longer to read than it takes to read the comic itself, precisely because most comic readers understand and process "regular layout" in an unthinking, instantaneous way.

Comic scholar Barbara Postema tells us, "Comics signal their reading process, time and again changing the rules of how they are to be read, but simultaneously offering a manual for how to approach them."[115] In short, comics teach readers how to read them. This claim, perhaps paradoxically, becomes clearer if one considers "alternative" or "experimental" comics that embrace narrative and formal complexities. Postema points to such creators as Richard McGuire, Rebecca Dart, Ben Katchor, and Chris Ware, who make long-form comics that stray from such conventions as chronological storytelling; regular, same-sized rectangular panels; and normal page reading patterns that move from left to right and from top to bottom. Such creators embrace multiple time frames (sometimes on the same page); wide variance in panel shape and size (occasionally abandoning panels altogether); and strange, winding patterns that might move in different directions over the course of a story (perhaps jumping across pages, or moving backward or in circles across pages). Comics like these, with "unconventional reading patterns [that] can become quite challenging," must offer some guidance to readers, whether it be the schemata that Chris Ware offers on the inside dust jacket of *Jimmy Corrigan: The Smartest Kid on Earth* or the way that *The Plant Book* "performs how the plant grows as the panels and pages grow in size too," to cite two of Postema's examples.[116] Without this guidance, such comics run the risk of seeming too difficult or obscure for casual readers.

At first glance, such guidance might not seem necessary for "regular" daily comics that tell their brief stories in three or four, left to right, rectangular panels that offer first a setup and then a punch line. Olivia Jaimes's *Nancy* looks simple. Jaimes draws the strip in a style that most readers will recognize as "cartoonish." The characters have simplified, easily readable facial features made of dots and a few curved lines; the setting is minimal, often just a table, desk, or couch if the strip takes place indoors or a tree, a bush, and some grass if it takes place outdoors. Objects like phones and computers are drawn simply as rectangles. Backgrounds are minimal, often as basic as a line marking the space between floor and wall or ground and sky, with each panel serving as a frame that marks the space of the strip. Despite this ease with which *Nancy* can be read (it might take all of three seconds to read a daily strip), I want to argue that Postema's claim that comics must offer structural guidance to readers holds true for *Nancy* (and while outside the scope of this study, for many, perhaps even all, other comics). Readers need *Nancy* to show us how to read *Nancy*. To return to Postema's language, even an easy-to-read strip like *Nancy* requires "a manual for how to approach" it. *Nancy* itself is that manual, showing readers the complex self-reflexivity, depth of character, social commentary, and formal experimentation that lies within its conventionally rectangular, everyday panels.[117] My claim here is not that *Nancy* reads itself or that it tells readers exactly what they should get from it. Rather, *Nancy* rewards close, careful reading and rereading. Jaimes's *Nancy* does many things and will do different things for different readers (if you doubt this, please consider the wide variance in readers' responses to *Nancy* discussed in chapter 2). In fact, the different ways that readers encounter Jaimes's strip both mark and perhaps help to account for its success. *Nancy* works as a flexible, relatable comic strip through its creator's persona, its representational strategies, and its humor, as I will discuss in the subsequent three chapters of this book, ending with a final chapter that shows how *Nancy* reflects on the ongoing COVID-19 pandemic.

Why *Nancy*?

Before describing each chapter, I want to say a few more words about why Jaimes's *Nancy* can be read as an archetype for contemporary flexible, relatable comic strips. While Olivia Jaimes comes from the world of webcomics, she also has the backing of Andrews McMeel Syndicate, so her creator persona can be a bit more distant from her readers. Most obviously, she writes using a pseudonym, which serves to keep her personal life separate from her work life. McMeel sells official *Nancy* merchandise, including pins, posters, and T-shirts, in its webstore, so Jaimes does not have to sell merchandise on her own like many webcomic creators do. And perhaps most importantly, Jaimes's editor, Shena Wolf, acts as a filter between Jaimes and the strip's readers. Michael Cavna writes that Jaimes has a "protective policy," summed up by Jaimes as "read no comments or coverage but occasionally be spoon-fed nice things other people have said by my editor."[118] The need for such a filter is no small thing. Many women comic creators have been attacked online. Hilary B. Price, in her afterword to Jaimes's first collection of *Nancy* comic strips, writes specifically of Jaimes's pseudonymity: "Being known as the new *Nancy* invites unwanted attention, and the internet is not the safest neighborhood to live in."[119] Jaimes's engagement with her audience is much more strategic than she lets on. As a flexible creator, Jaimes can relate to print and legacy readers through creating a strong connection to previous iterations of *Nancy*. Jaimes's *Nancy* is instantly recognizable as the *Nancy* created by Ernie Bushmiller over eighty years ago, in both form and content. Jaimes draws Nancy's pointy black hair, red bow, white shirt, and red-and-black polka-dot skirt much as Bushmiller did; the strip is three or four panels, with a punch line that is often a play on words or an illustration of Nancy's obstinacy.

With the critical and commercial success of *Nancy* over the past three years, King Features Syndicate seems to be trying to replicate the model that Andrews McMeel took in hiring a webcomic creator to take over a legacy strip. On October 12, 2020, the webcartoonist Jules Rivera—creator of *Love, Jules*—took over the job of writing and drawing the legacy comic *Mark Trail*. Like the press attention given to Jaimes's reboot of *Nancy*, Rivera's reboot received much attention from the comic press online and was even the subject of a *New York Times* article. While daily comic strips do not get much mainstream press coverage, reboots of classic strips by webcomic creators seem to warrant interest. Leading up to Rivera's reboot, King Features followed the *Nancy*-reboot playbook. They published an interview with Rivera online, and a long YouTube interview was uploaded after Rivera's first *Mark Trail* strips were published. Instead of calling her work on *Mark Trail* a reboot, "she describes it as a 'blowup,' a bigger focus on the characters and themes of the strip but with a modern sensibility, which let her put her degree in electrical engineering and a background in STEM to use."[120] King Features has also rebooted the legacy strip *Flash Gordon* as an "all-new, original comic strip anthology project" with forty different creators, "from your favorite funny page cartoonists to top comic book artists, animators, graphic novelists and web cartoonists," writing strips that will appear "in both print and digital formats."[121] In addition, King Features published an online poll on November 9, 2020, asking readers which legacy comic strip they would like to see rebooted, including *Krazy Kat*, *Apartment 3-G*, and *Popeye*. As syndicated daily comics cross-pollinate with webcomics, Jaimes's *Nancy* serves as an exemplar of contemporary flexible daily comics.

In addition, Michelle Ann Abate, in her *Funny Girls: Guffaws, Guts, and Gender in Classic American Comics*, has noted that "the number of female comics characters, fans, and creators increased exponentially" in the twenty-first century.[122] For Abate, whose work on Bushmiller's *Nancy* I discuss in chapter 2 of this book, this recent increase harkens back to an early twentieth-century forgotten golden age of girl characters in American comics. Jaimes's *Nancy* clearly becomes a part of this tradition and begins the process of creating a more representative daily comics "page," whether in print newspapers or online on GoComics and Comics Kingdom. Hilary B. Price notes that there are very few well-known daily comic strips "whose title and author are female names" currently in print, citing *Mary Worth*'s writer Karen Moy and artist June Brigman as one of the few current examples.[123] When Moy and Brigman teamed up in 2016, they became the first all-women team to produce *Mary Worth* since 1939.[124] Cathy Guisewite revived her retired daily strip *Cathy* as the single-panel, five-days-a-week *Cathy Commiserations* on March 8, 2020, but the number of women creators writing and drawing female title characters remains quite small. Jaimes's *Nancy* takes on significance as one of the few such syndicated strips to appear in print and online. Even as daily comics have diversified in recent years, the twentieth-century baseline assumption that newspaper comics were by white male creators for white audiences who wanted to see "universal" white characters has changed quite slowly.

Chapter Descriptions

Chapter 1 begins with Nancy's plan to be "an inspirational lifestyle blogger." In this chapter, I argue that Jaimes incorporates both her webcomic past and her legacy-strip present into a flexible and relatable authorial persona. *Nancy* and other flexible strips that appear both digitally and in print inhabit an online space of constant feedback, anonymous commentary, and engaged reading. Jaimes blurs the line between life and work and confronts the precarity of working in daily comics in the twenty-first century. I detail the kinds of digital labor that webcomic creators perform to market their comics and build connections with fans. This work is a kind of emotional or affective labor to create relatability. "Olivia Jaimes" is a pseudonym; behind this name, Jaimes performs her digital labor with a self-reflexive irony. The connections that Jaimes builds with her readers mimic the close connection to readers that webcomic creators strive for. At the same time, her pseudonymity puts a barrier between Jaimes and her readers. Because *Nancy* also appears in print and since it is a legacy comic, Jaimes must also perform certain kinds of labor directed toward these aspects of the strip. In essence, *Nancy* has two audiences: nostalgic readers immersed in the strip's past and newer readers who engage the strip online. As a flexible creator, Jaimes relates to both of these audiences. Her working persona becomes part of the content of *Nancy*, as she blurs the lines between Nancy the character, "the artist" who often appears in the strip, and Jaimes herself. Jaimes uses a visual language that shows readers the online space that Nancy inhabits. Nancy and her friends constantly look at phone and laptop screens, and Jaimes often draws the content that Nancy posts online. Through such techniques as empty speech balloons and repetitive images, Jaimes shows readers the online world of "confidence culture" that both Nancy the character and *Nancy* the strip inhabit. The often invisible labor of creating content and relating to readers becomes visible as readers follow Nancy's and Jaimes's struggles to become famous.

Chapter 2 begins with a discussion of Jaimes's redesign of Nancy's aunt Fritzi. Fritzi was designed in the 1920s as a sex symbol who wore short skirts and tight-fitting clothes. Both within and outside the strip, Fritzi served as an object of the male gaze. Her character design remained largely unchanged until Jaimes's reboot. Jaimes anticipated readers' negative reactions to her "new" Fritzi and directly addressed them in the strip by portraying Fritzi in bulky snowsuits. I discuss how Jaimes keeps a safe distance from fans while engaging fan commentary in the strip and focus on the small but dedicated fan communities of *Nancy*. A very small but vocal subset of fans (nostalgic, mostly male readers) shows how virulent misogyny can become in fan communities, so Jaimes's decision to not read online comments makes sense, as does her decision to write the strip under a pseudonym. I discuss how other flexible creators, such as Jules Rivera, engage fans differently and sometimes more directly. Keeping audience engagement in mind, this chapter looks at the ways Jaimes configures gender and race in her characters. Following Michelle Ann Abate's work on the history of girl comic characters, I discuss how Jaimes confronts *Nancy*'s legacy of representations of gender and race. Abate convincingly argues that Bushmiller's *Nancy* is rooted in an early American tradition of vaudeville and minstrelsy. Bushmiller's *Nancy* likewise followed mid-twentieth-century ideals of romantic love, with Nancy and Sluggo portrayed as a couple who would eventually marry. Much of the strip's humor lay in Nancy's jealousy of Sluggo's attention to other girls. Jaimes shifts these gender relations in her reboot. Rather than focus on romantic feelings between Sluggo and Nancy, Jaimes focuses on how technology-mediated female friendship works in the twenty-first century. Jaimes shares this focus with other contemporary webcomics and flexible comics such as Enzo's *Cheer Up, Emo Kid*, Cassandra Calin's *Cassandra Comics*, Shen T.'s *Shen's Comics*, and Sarah Andersen's *Sarah's Scribbles*. In different ways, all of these comics address the materiality of fan communities and the importance of relatability.

Jaimes also confronts the history of racism that haunts newspaper comics. Until the 1960s, newspaper comic strips often used racist stereotypes in their representations of nonwhite characters. Morrie Turner created *Wee Pals* in 1965, in part to bring "more Black characters to the funny pages."[125] Only five newspapers picked up the strip, "because many newspapers refused to run a strip featuring Black characters."[126] It took three years for *Wee Pals* to get full syndication and become the "the first comic strip syndicated in the United States featuring a diverse ethnic cast."[127] During the civil rights era, white comic creators struggled to introduce Black characters into predominately white comic strips. Charles Schulz's 1968 introduction of Franklin, the first Black character in *Peanuts*, serves as an exemplar of how comics slowly began to change in the 1960s. Franklin's introduction was met with death threats and threatened boycotts, but the character also served as inspiration for young Black readers who would go on to create comic strips that centered Black characters, including Robert Armstrong, creator of *Jump Start*. In the 1990s and 2000s, more Black creators achieved syndication with comics focusing on Black characters, such as Aaron McGruder's *Boondocks*, Ted Shearer's *Quincy*, Stephen Bentley's *Herb and Jamal*, and Ray Billingsley's *Curtis*. But as Sheena C. Howard noted in 2015, "the funny pages are still only peppered with representations of African American comic strips."[128] White comic strip characters, Rebecca Wanzo argues, remain the norm: "Idealized white children, as pictured in comic strips such as *Peanuts*, *Family [Circus]*, or *Archie*, are ideal in their average travails."[129]

Ernie Bushmiller resisted including Black characters in *Nancy*, because he thought their inclusion would not add to the strip's humor. Black characters in daily comic strips remain relatively rare today, but Jaimes has created a racially diverse cast of characters in Nancy's friends and teachers and in background characters. More importantly, Jaimes illustrates how racial representations matter on the page and screen, as her characters often create and draw their own characters within the strip. Through these representations, readers can see that Nancy and her friends have an awareness of racial difference, even as that awareness plays only a small part in their characterization.

Chapter 3 focuses on the ways that humor works in contemporary flexible comic strips like *Nancy*. Chapters 1 and 2 argue that the material conditions of Jaimes's persona, *Nancy*'s fandom, and the strip's history all shape the strip in important ways. Chapter 3 argues that *Nancy*'s humor is likewise grounded in the material conditions of both the contemporary world and the strip's history. I argue that such humor is often object based and that the objects of humor can be broadly divided into two categories: "old" objects such as cookie jars and "new" objects such as Snapchat filters. This chapter maps out a theory of object-based humor following Graham Harman's discussion of humor as a kind of allure or attraction to objects. The cookie jar has a long history of being just such an object of humor in comic strips, since the 1940s, in strips like Charles Schulz's *Peanuts*, Mort Walker's *Hi and Lois*, Jim Davis's *Garfield*, and Bill Watterson's *Calvin and Hobbes*. All these strips create humor by depicting characters' strong desire for the forbidden contents of cookie jars. Jaimes continues this tradition in a series of strips where Nancy creates elaborate schemes to reach a cookie jar placed on a high shelf or on top of a refrigerator. This type of humor, focused on old nostalgic objects, continues to resonate with readers, even as cookie jars have been relegated to the space of antique collectibles in the real world. At the same time, Jaimes and other contemporary creators use new technological objects such as smart phones, laptops, and the iconography of social media to create humor firmly rooted in the present. Comics like Nathan Pyle's *Strange Planet* and Sarah Andersen's *Sarah's Scribbles* base much of their humor in screens and on things like the heart-shaped "like" icon prevalent on social media. Flexible creators like Jaimes rely on both nostalgic objects and contemporary technological objects to produce humor. Even as Jaimes bases jokes partially on readers' ability to recognize things like Wikipedia entries, she also uses metahumor to connect with readers. Metahumor is as old as the earliest newspaper comic strips, so nostalgic readers are well aware of the conventions of breaking the fourth wall and directly addressing readers. At the same time, Jaimes and other creators show how metacomics are materially grounded in the objects of their times. Midcentury comic creators used pens and drawing tables to create metahumor, whereas contemporary creators use web filters and screens to produce metahumor. Metahumor, then, is always rooted in specific cultural and material concerns. Contemporary flexible creators like Jaimes use metahumor to explore how technology-mediated subjectivity works in the twenty-first century.

Finally, chapter 4 focuses on how *Nancy* has addressed the COVID-19 pandemic that started early in 2020. *Nancy* addresses the materiality of the pandemic, including mask wearing, social distancing, remote learning, and videoconferencing. The strip explores how the pandemic has changed characters' subjectivities as they relate to surveillance technologies and other mediations made prominent during periods of isolation. Daily newspaper comics have a built-in lag time of several weeks, so they sometimes have difficulty addressing contemporary issues. Many daily comics have ignored the pandemic. Webcomics do not have the same lag time, and many have directly addressed the pandemic. As a flexible comic strip, *Nancy* has subtly adapted to real-world lockdowns and social distancing. In the strip, school has been moved online, and Aunt Fritzi has been working from home since April 2020. While the pandemic is never directly mentioned, *Nancy*'s focus on screens, video chats, and other forms of technology-mediated subjectivity make it easy for the strip to relate to changes in the real world. In its response to these events, *Nancy* and other like-minded strips and webcomics illustrate the importance of social and cultural materiality to the understanding of flexible comics. Twenty-first-century comics help to make sense of the world and only make sense as a part of the world.

One final introductory note: As you read this book, you will notice that each chapter begins with a specific *Nancy* strip. For production reasons, only one strip is reproduced per chapter. When I discuss other *Nancy* strips, I always give the date of publication. All of Olivia Jaimes's *Nancy* comics can be read at GoComics, where they are searchable by date, so readers can easily find each strip I reference.

2. *Nancy*, by Olivia Jaimes, November 8, 2019. NANCY © 2019. Reprinted by permission of ANDREWS MCMEEL SYNDICATION for UFS. All rights reserved.

1

"Cash Preferred"

Olivia Jaimes's Working Persona (November 8, 2019)

Nancy as Lifestyle Blogger

On October 15, 2019, Nancy declares that she is "an inspirational lifestyle blogger." Over the next few months, numerous strips depict Nancy staring at her laptop and developing strategies to gain more followers. On November 8, 2019, in a large panel that takes up more than half the strip, Nancy writes a blog post that begins, "Dear Blog Readers: Today I ate some _____ and drank some _____ and then I put on my _____ shoes and my _____ backpack." The post continues in this manner, with blank lines where brand names might go. The final two panels comprise an "Artist's Note" written in white text on a black background. No images appear in these two panels, only text. These two panels of pure text are meant to be a sort of metacommentary in which Olivia Jaimes directly addresses readers. She writes to those who are wondering why there are blank spaces in Nancy's blog post and refers to "the panel before this one" to make abundantly clear that she is referring to the action taking place in the strip. Readers are meant to read the gutter between the first and second panel as a time of reflection, when "the artist" considered exactly why she left blanks in Nancy's blog post—namely, that she does not want to give out "free advertising." The third panel contains the punch line in both a visual and textual manner. In terms of visual layout, there is no reason why the "Artist's Note" is not contained within one larger square panel to parallel the first panel. The third panel tells readers that it is "(cont.)" from the previous panel, signifying that the artist is using more space than originally planned, as if she is writing the strip in real time, with no opportunity to revise and fit the note into one panel. The textual payoff in panel 3 comes from a logical reversal. Readers will probably expect the artist to say why she does not want any company to get "free advertising." Instead, she writes, "I want *lots* of companies to **pay** for advertising from me!! Advertisers, these blank spaces could be yours!"

I want to note the obvious here—Jaimes is not actually asking advertisers for money. Nonetheless, this strip points to the precarious nature of making a living as a comic creator, bringing to mind Jaimes's advice regarding the difficulty of making a career in comics (as I discuss in the introduction), while also noting that many bloggers make money from sponsored content. Jaimes makes an interesting double conflation in this strip, first between Nancy the blogger and the "artist" and second between the "artist" and Olivia Jaimes. When the "artist" writes that readers might wonder why she "didn't put" brand names in the first panel, she points out the artifice of the strip, telling readers in essence that she writes Nancy's words. Jaimes also shows readers that Nancy is not able to get sponsored content for her blog. Further, readers may be led to think about the similarities between the "artist," who seeks money from advertisers, and Olivia Jaimes, who of course is paid to create *Nancy* but does not earn enough to make a career of it.

In calling out to advertisers, Jaimes harkens back to the early twentieth-century connection between the technical layout and the economic model of comic strips. As comic critic and historian Ian Gordon describes in *Comic Strips and Consumer Culture, 1890–1945*, there are material, historical reasons why the four-panel comic strip seems regular to readers. Gordon tells us that at the turn of the twentieth century, daily comics helped increase newspaper circulation and served as vehicles for advertisers. Gordon argues that comic strips had to be character driven, in order to encourage readers to follow the daily adventures in the comics and thus buy newspapers. As popular characters like the Katzenjammer Kids and Happy Hooligan were developed, creators invented many of the conventions that are still familiar to readers over a hundred years later: "Devices such as panels and word balloons worked to elaborate and extend these characters by placing them in narratives and supplying them with voices."[1] Such tools of sequential graphic narrative served a distinct purpose—the development of character. As Gordon notes, this development "laid the basis for widespread distribution of comic strips and development of the formal properties of the art form that later proved useful for advertising."[2] Characters drove the narrative and created a desire in readers to follow the actions of specific characters, which in turn gave these characters an identity that could be used to sell both newspapers and other products. In short, the sequential panels, word balloons, continuing stories, and central characters of comics came together in the early twentieth century as part of a commodity culture. Jaimes jokingly updates this inherited legacy to depict a twenty-first-century means of monetizing, where brands pay her for exposure in the strip and where Nancy hopes sponsors will pay to be mentioned on her blog.

But the call for advertising cash and sponsored content is not the only work-related joke in this strip, as it also says a lot about the connections between relatability, work, and digital culture. Akane Kanai, in *Gender and Relatability in Digital Culture: Managing Affect, Intimacy and Value*, notes that online work techniques create a "self [that] is made digitally distributable and relatable for a set of imagined others. Formulated as part of a branded relationship with others, there are resonances between this relatability and other accounts of the instrumentalisation of 'positive' affects."[3] Nancy, "the artist," and Olivia Jaimes all form a part of this self that relates to readers in a twenty-first-century digital economy that strives to find value wherever it can, whether in likes, readers, or actual cash. Jaimes's November 18 strip exemplifies the flexible materialism of contemporary comic strips in using traditional comic techniques to comment on the changing nature of work.

Jaimes uses Nancy's lifestyle blog to focus on the ways that branding can be digital work for real-world girls. Kanai writes that "girls and young women continue to figure as ideal consumer-entrepreneurs . . . uniting the production of desire and positive affects with brands and other consumer goods."[4] Nancy continually struggles to achieve internet fame yet remains ambitious and optimistic, paralleling Jaimes's work as a new creator fashioning her own voice for a legacy comic. Nancy continually has difficulty generating content for her lifestyle blog, so she employs various tricks to gain followers, adding clickbait (November 15, 2019) and then more hashtags (November 21, 2019). On November 29 she realizes that she can insert filler instead of generating more content. Sluggo asks her who will continue reading her blog once they realize it is all filler. The third panel shows Nancy's face in the bottom left corner of the panel, with a large word balloon filling the rest of the panel. The words "Oh, I'm sure" fill the center of the balloon, but most of the panel is white. The fourth panel shows only a quarter of Nancy's face and an even larger word balloon that fills nearly the whole panel but contains only the words "someone will." With these exaggerated word balloons and minimal text, Jaimes graphically performs Nancy's claim. The speech bubbles fill the strip with emptiness, but someone still reads it. In fact, as of

October 18, 2020, this strip has forty-nine likes and seventeen comments on GoComics. (Icons for comments, likes, and pins and for sharing on Facebook and Twitter are always visible to the right of any comic on GoComics.) Katherine Kelp-Stebbins, in "Reading Spaces: The Politics of Page Layout," writes that comics "may be representations of space and spaces of representation simultaneously."[5] The exaggerated speech balloons of January 23 exemplify this idea. The balloons literally fill the space of the last two panels so that nothing else can be drawn in those panels. The white space of the speech bubble becomes a part of the strip's diegetic space—that is, what Pascal Lefèvre calls "the fictive space in which the characters live and act."[6] Within the frame of the panel, the empty white space represents the contentless nature of Nancy's blog and of the November 29 comic itself.

At the same time, Jaimes creates a "space of representation," showing Nancy's desire to occupy the kind of digital space where she can build a #relatable, branded connection with others, as described by Kanai. The speech bubble thus functions as an extradiegetic space—that is, "the space outside the fictive world of the comic."[7] Readers can see precisely the digital space of online work as a blank space to be filled with #relatable content. In a similar vein, Jaimes's December 13, 2019, strip makes a joke connecting contentless internet comments to the strip itself while also illustrating Nancy's desire to be an influencer. The first two panels of this four-panel strip show Lyle, a classmate of Nancy's, looking at a laptop screen and complaining that all the comments on Nancy's blog are just bots talking to each other. He asks Nancy, "Who wants to read what two fake people caught in a loop are saying?" The third panel shifts perspective slightly so that we can see Nancy sitting next to Lyle. She replies, "Lots of people," to which her friend says, "No they don't." The fourth panel is visually identical to the third, except for the words in the speech balloons. Nancy responds, "Yes, they do," and her classmate repeats, "No they don't." The repetition from panel 3 to panel 4 represents the feedback loop that the friend critiques, as readers find themselves reading "two fake people" saying the same thing. Still, Nancy's obstinate defense that people do indeed want to read bots commenting to each other speaks to her desire to be part of this discourse, and Jaimes once again visualizes the space of this discourse, this time through the use of repeated images from panel 3 to panel 4. Earlier in this story line, when Nancy laments to Sluggo that she may never become an internet superstar (November 2, 2019), he tells her that her problem is that she does not "have a marketing team paying an algorithm to boost" her likes. Rather than taking this advice as a reason not to worry about how many likes she has, Nancy writes a blog post that begins, "The solution to my problems was to drink more [name brand] soda." Nancy wants to brand herself because she hopes it will generate more likes and perhaps money.

While the humor of the strip lies in the way that Nancy responds to Sluggo's advice, what he says makes sense. On her own, Nancy would have a hard time becoming "an inspirational lifestyle blogger." Sluggo's mention of a marketing team can serve to remind us that Olivia Jaimes does have such a marketing team in Andrews McMeel Syndicate. Likewise, as a legacy comic nearly one hundred years old, *Nancy* is a brand name. Both of these points contribute to Jaimes's persona. At the same time, it is worth remembering that Jaimes has her roots in making webcomics, as these roots also contribute to her persona.

Building a Persona

In "Scott Pilgrim vs the Future of Comics Publishing," Padmini Ray Murray notes that webcomics "emerged as a consequence of comic creators wishing to indulge their artistic freedom in a climate where increasingly risk-averse comic publishers were unwilling to take a chance on more adventurous approaches to comic making."[8] With publishers unwilling to take a chance on certain comics, the financial risks fall to the creator. Murray notes that webcomics are often free to view online, so the "viability of webcomics is not assured; more often than not comic creators make more money on merchandise associated with the comic (sometimes, in a strange reversal, this may be the print version of the webcomic) and advertising, rather than the comic itself."[9] Webcomic creators must do more work than just create and publish their comic. They must "create intimate relationships with their readerships that often grew and sustained their support" through sharing information on such things as "their artistic process online, often blogging about their method in detail, and communicating with their readers regarding creative decisions made."[10] Webcomic creators also often generate supplemental content to gain and keep their readers' attention. Nathan Pyle, who has achieved commercial success with his webcomic *Strange Planet*, exemplifies this type of work. When Pyle posts a new *Strange Planet* strip on Instagram (@nathanpylestrangeplanet), which he does on a near-daily basis, he includes ads for merchandise and additional, free non–*Strange Planet* comics that he has created. These comics are often drawn simply, such as the four-panel "Me as a Giraffe" that he posted on October 21, 2020, which shows a giraffe head munching on leaves in all four panels. He has also published humorous short videos of pigeons foraging, with captions added like "Charles get a bread" (October 18, 2020) so that the birds seem to be engaged in conversation. Pyle has even posted a tutorial about the editing tool he uses to make these videos. Pyle is also active on Twitter (@nathanwpyle), where he interacts with fans and posts about things like watching baseball games.

The digital work done by webcomic creators like Pyle is a kind of emotional or affective labor, a self-production meant to relate to readers, to form emotional bonds. Akane Kanai argues that "this outward-oriented self-production requires strategic use of feelings and personal experience to facilitate the formation of collectivities around affective sameness. . . . The relaying of everyday intimacy becomes a constitutive part of branded practices precisely because of its engendering of feelings of proximity and sameness."[11] Put more crassly, one could say that emotion sells merchandise. But webcomic creators who want to make a career of comics must do this kind of labor. Malcolm Harris writes that "affective labor (or feeling work) engages . . . the innate capacities and practices that distinguish our species, like language and games and mutual understanding."[12] Performing affective labor means becoming #relatable. A defining characteristic of webcomics is just this relatability. Flexible creators must create #relatable online personas and create #relatable comics. In "A Historical Approach to Webcomics: Digital Authorship in the Early 2000s," Leah Misemer argues that crowdfunding has become "one of the most major shifts for webcomics, [and] helps cartoonists supplement the money they make from selling material goods. The 2013 emergence of Patreon . . . has had a particularly strong impact and has enabled a large number of webcomics authors to make cartooning a full-time job."[13] Importantly, as Misemer notes, crowdfunding and social media are deeply intertwined: "Crowdfunding owes its success to another major digital shift since 2007: the rise of social media."[14] Social media create the spaces for digital affective labor, and by creating the possibility of becoming successful through self-publishing, social media help create the need for affective labor. Writing of the newfound technical ease that aids the production and distribution of creative works, Harris claims, "You no longer need to go to a label or a studio to make a market-ready album, music video, movie, or television show. . . . But to reap the rewards, you're going to need to beat almost everyone else just like you."[15] In other words, when anyone can create and post music, film, novels, shows, or comics, it becomes nearly impossible for any single creative work to gain attention. Without a marketing department, creators like Nancy (to be clear, I mean Jaimes's fictional character here) need to "drink more [name brand] soda" than their fellow creators.

Jaimes herself performs little of this affective digital labor. Rather, she incorporates it into her strip through both Nancy's character and through "the artist" who occasionally addresses readers of the strip. In essence, Jaimes places two barriers— Nancy and "the artist"—between herself and readers. Many webcomic creators do not employ such barriers as they seek to create connections with readers. Sean Kleefeld argues that connecting with readers is a condition of possibility for webcomics: "It's almost necessary for a creator to interact with their readers" through social media to engender loyalty.[16] Kleefeld writes, "To be a fan of a webcomic is to be a fan of its creator, and vice versa."[17] In keeping a further distance from her readers, Jaimes reminds readers that while *Nancy* embraces many of the conventions of webcomics, it is a legacy syndicated strip that appears both online and in daily newspapers. *Nancy* brings attention to the kinds of work required of comic creators as they adapt to changing methods of comic delivery and consumption. Flexible comics like *Nancy* reflect on the societal need for affective digital labor, and this reflection helps shape the style and content of flexible comics. Misemer asks that we "consider how else webcomics might reflect how technology shapes digital media."[18] We might also ask how digital media, specifically comics, reflect and shape technology *and* how all these things work together to produce subjects that can live in this world.

Partially, these questions are considerations of style. As the editors of *The Best American Comics, 2014*, Scott McCloud and Bill Kartalopoulos felt compelled to include webcomics in their curated collection. In a section titled "Oh Crap—Webcomics!" McCloud writes, "Webcomics and their possibilities are never far from my mind."[19] McCloud notes the same flexibility that Aaron Kashtan names and that I have been focusing on: "The boundaries between print and Web were important to my tribe of inventors, but today those boundaries have blurred beyond recognition."[20] I am more interested, though, in what McCloud has to say about the style of webcomics. McCloud writes that "standards of excellence in cartooning . . . may be violently rewritten from time to time, and a long list of artistic prerequisites ripped to pieces." In 2014 he saw digital comics fomenting such a reordering of standards. He writes that "some of the most popular new webcomics of the last decade are also some of the most radically stripped down or dissonant in appearance and style."[21] For McCloud, webcomics like Randal Munroe's *xkcd* "offer a deceptively simple, even crude, outer appearance"; McCloud says that Allie Brosh's webcomics "may be the most jarring to traditional sensibilities, with [their] sloppy, scribbly style."[22] McCloud seems accurate in his description of the style of webcomics. Many look simple and sloppy, with minimal backgrounds. The abovementioned *Strange Planet* features blobby, humanoid, nameless main characters. Alex Norris's *Webcomic Name* features humanoid blobs and poorly drawn animals that become recognizable only when a name is attached to them. Sarah Andersen's *Sarah's Scribbles* names the drawing style of her characters, who usually appear against a featureless background. Many webcomics pay little attention to backgrounds, thus giving little geographic specificity to their work.

Nancy's status as a legacy comic strip limits Jaimes's drawing style. Nancy and Sluggo must be recognizable to readers; there has to be a certain amount of visual continuity with the strip's history. While Jaimes introduces numerous new characters and completely redesigns Nancy's aunt Fritzi,[23] the strip's main characters would be recognizable to a reader who last saw the strip in the 1940s. Nancy's outfit and spiky hair, as well as Sluggo's bald head, cap, and threadbare clothing, remain largely the same as they were during the Bushmiller era. At the same time, Jaimes does use certain stylistic devices common to webcomics. In my introduction I refer to the simplified facial features, minimal settings and backgrounds, and basically wrought objects as "cartoonish," but they could just as easily be described as "web-cartoonish." Like many webcomics, Jaimes's *Nancy* does not take place in a recognizable locale. Emotions are displayed with a few lines. The strip is legible whether read on a three-inch phone screen or a large computer monitor. Just as Jaimes has made Nancy's desire to be an influencer part of her own persona, she has also reflected on her own drawing style and artistic talent through Nancy, as well as through the character of the artist.

In a series of comics from 2019, Nancy decides that she wants to become famous. In the February 11, 2019, strip, Nancy tells Aunt Fritzi, "I want to be famous without having to do any work." She develops two plans that play out over numerous strips. First, she decides she will be a famous artist. On February 25 she asks her friend Agnes, who is a good artist, for advice. Agnes tells Nancy, in a series of strips (including March 9 and 11), that creating good art and building an online following takes a lot of work and time. Lucy, Agnes's twin sister, suggests that Nancy make her art "relatable," as "people respond to seeing their own experiences reflected in art" (March 26). Nancy then draws a stick-figure self-portrait with a smaller figure looking at her. The smaller figure has the word "jealous" scribbled over its head. Nancy is oblivious to the amateur quality of her own art. Instead, she decides that her audience must be envious of her talent. A few days later, Nancy reaches the conclusion that people "can't relate to me through my art because I'm too awesome" (April 8).

This series of strips shows that Nancy believes that internet fame should be instant and unrelated to the quality of work or effort. Kanai provides some interesting ways of thinking about Nancy's desire for fame. Kanai writes, "In contemporary digital life, we may observe that young women in influencer, lifestyle and micro-celebrity work are labouring to produce a seamless account of the self to digital audiences in which the intimate and the commercial are deeply entwined."[24] Nancy fails to become an influential artist because she refuses to put in the labor required. Nancy's laziness can be read as satiric— her desire for fame is banal and empty—but also as somewhat ironic. Nancy's failure itself becomes #relatable to readers who might idly dream of internet fame, which in turns helps Jaimes's strip to gain popularity directly through its relatability. Nancy's confidence in the face of failure exemplifies what Kanai sees as a conflation of girlishness and salesmanship: "In a neoliberal conjuncture where the image of youthful femininity is 'condensed' with that of the ideal entrepreneurial subject, certain dispositions are privileged [including] affective orientations that may be deemed 'positive,' such as ambition and optimism, converting negative experiences into feel good outcomes."[25] Nancy quits posting art, but she doesn't worry about it, because she will come up with another entrepreneurial plan. She buys into what Kanai calls the "confidence culture" of lifestyle marketing.[26] Nancy knows her art deserves fame but believes her audience is not yet ready for her talent.

In contrast with Nancy's inability to find an online audience, Olivia Jaimes had a built-in audience with the publication of her first *Nancy* strip. With the backing of her syndicate's marketers, Jaimes was guaranteed a certain number of readers from the start. Within the strip, though, Jaimes has maintained a certain level of ambiguity about her own artistic talent through continued references to "the artist" and her drawing abilities. On March 5, 2019, Agnes offers Nancy some practical art advice. She tells Nancy to "add sunglasses" if she's made a mistake drawing eyes; to "just make it bigger" if you draw a mouth wrong; and if everything goes wrong, "just scribble it all out and add a label." In each panel, we see Agnes carry out this advice as she corrects her own drawings. The fourth panel shows Jaimes taking Agnes's advice. The panel comprises a usual drawing of Nancy's head and upper body, with a speech balloon above her head. Instead of Nancy's eyes, we see a pair of scribbled-on sunglasses; instead of her normal mouth line, we see a much wider drawn mouth. The speech bubble is completely scribbled out in black lines, with the word "punchline" and an arrow pointing to the speech bubble drawn directly below it. Similarly, on July 9, 2020, Aunt Fritzi shows Nancy the rings on a tree stump. Rather than the expected comments about what the size of the rings can tell us about the tree's growth, Fritzi points to an uneven circle and says, "These rings are from when the artist was bad at drawing circles." Like Nancy, though, Jaimes shows confidence in her art despite the misgivings the "artist" shows in many strips. Both Nancy and Jaimes build their personas through jokes about confidence. Jaimes includes a signed note as the first panel of her December 22, 2018, strip. The note begins, "Happy Holidays, Readers!" and offers a gift of thanks: "I've redrawn some of my favorite illustrations from this past year for you to use as profile pictures, avatars, or art for the walls of your home. PLEASE ENJOY!!" The redrawn art includes a white "cloud," a "bush" drawn exactly the same shape as the cloud but colored green, a "bush (with berries)" that adds black dots to the previous drawing, a "thought bubble" that looks exactly like the cloud, a new character's "hair" that looks exactly like the cloud except it is orange, and an orange "bush." Jaimes seems to be taking to heart what Nancy said she learned at art camp, in the August 13, 2018, strip: "I learned that negative self-talk is one of your greatest foes as you begin your artistic journey."

Regarding Jaimes's "artistic journey," I note in my introduction that Jaimes suggests that making comics might not be a good career choice. After this claim, she says, "You don't have to make the thing you love your job."[27] Jaimes uses a similar line in the strip on February 23, 2019. After Nancy tells her teacher that wants to be an artist, her teacher replies, "Just because you like something doesn't mean you should make it your job." The teacher uses cake as a metaphor, telling Nancy that even though you like cake, you wouldn't want to have a job eating cake every day "even if you weren't hungry." Rather than taking this lesson to heart, Nancy replies, "You're right. That cake eating job would be a much better fit for me." Nancy remains an entrepreneur. She continually works to monetize her writing and her lifestyle.

The Labor of Comic Creation

While Jaimes has kept her other job, she has continually explored what it means to work as a comic creator in her strips. A small part of this exploration can be seen in the evolution of Jaimes's signature over the first month or so of the strip. An artist's signature serves as a written symbol of their work, and many signatures have become iconic, such as R. Crumb's and Charles Schulz's. Likewise, many comic strip creators handwrite the date on each of their strips. As "Olivia Jaimes" is a pseudonym,

Jaimes had to invent her signature. In her first *Nancy* strip, Jaimes prints her full name and writes the date after it. Within a month (on May 7, 2018, to be exact), Jaimes began to sign the strips with the initials "OJ," followed by the date. On May 14 the stylized cursive signature that Jaimes has stuck with first appears. Sunday strips have to be finished weeks or even a month in advance of their publication. Jaimes's early Sunday strips (through May 27, 2018) are unsigned, and the date, with day and month only, is typed, not handwritten. Jaimes's signature appears with a typed full date next to it for the next two weeks, before she standardizes to signature and handwritten date on June 17, 2018.

Of course, Jaimes is not the only comic creator to be self-reflective. In fact, Ernie Bushmiller himself had a running Labor Day gag that he, as a cartoonist, should have a day free from creating the strip. Bushmiller would do things like draw a cloud of smoke that hid all but Nancy's and Sluggo's legs, with Nancy saying, while pointing to Bushmiller's signature in the lower corner of the panel, "He doesn't want to draw us today—less work on Labor Day" (September 5, 1960). In other Labor Day strips, Nancy and Sluggo refer to Bushmiller as the "Boss." To make the strip easier for him to draw, Nancy and Sluggo go swimming under water so only the tops of their heads appear (September 1, 1969). In another Labor Day strip (September 3, 1973), Nancy and Sluggo become a "rubber stamp" pressed to the page, and the rubber-stamped Nancy says, "Our boss refused to draw us on Labor Day." Even as Bushmiller portrays himself as the boss of his characters, he reminds readers that cartooning is work and thus should be rewarded a day off, just like other forms of labor.

Jaimes has continued this tradition in the three Labor Day strips she has created so far, reminding readers that cartooning is still labor, even if it is a different kind of work than when

Bushmiller was earning a living with *Nancy*. Jaimes never portrays herself as the "boss" of her characters. Each of Jaimes's Labor Day strips starts with an "Artist Note," and on Labor Day September 3, 2018, and September 7, 2020, Jaimes started the note with the same sentence: "It's Labor Day, so I'm taking the day off." On September 2, 2019, she writes, "Since it's Labor Day, my editors have agreed to let me take it easy." Of course, comics are not created on the day they are published, so the very idea of not working on Labor Day for a cartoonist is a joke. And Jaimes amplifies the artifice of this joke each year. In 2018 she wrote, "Please enjoy this sneak peek at panels that will be appearing in upcoming strips," and in 2020 she wrote, "I'll be looking back through the archives to revisit some stand-out panels from the last year of *Nancy*." Neither strip does what it promises. The "future" panels that appear in the 2018 strip are not from actual strips.[28] The "archival" panels from the 2020 strip are repetitions of the "Artist Note" that makes up the first panel.[29] In her 2019 Labor Day strip, Jaimes offers an ironic critique of her own art. In the "Artist Note," she writes, "Most days, I work pretty hard to match the look and feel of classic *Nancy*." But as her editors are letting her take it easy for the holiday, Jaimes writes that she will "draw a strip in my natural style." The next three panels show Nancy drawn in the style of *Prince Valiant*, a comic that in many ways is the antithesis of *Nancy*. Started in 1937 by Hal Foster, *Prince Valiant* was a full-page, color, Sunday-only comic (that is still published today, even though Foster died in 1982). It is an epic story based in Arthurian legend. Brian Walker writes that Foster "designed spectacular panels filled with battling warriors, galloping horses, towering castles, and panoramic scenery."[30] Foster once said that he spent fifty-three hours per week working on the strip. Jaimes mimics both the art and writing of Foster's work. The panel that shows Nancy and the dropped ice cream reads,

"Nancy stares in despair at the ice cream she has so recently lost." *Prince Valiant*, with its elaborate style, has little in common with webcomic-style art and storytelling.

While Jaimes says she has worked hard to emulate classic *Nancy*, she keeps her relationship to it ambiguous. The back matter of Jaimes's *Nancy: A Comic Collection* includes a section called "Fan Art of *Nancy* by Olivia Jaimes." In the nine full-page drawings that appear in "Fan Art," Jaimes draws Nancy in different styles, including *Nancy with a Pearl Earring*, echoing Vermeer's famous painting; *Nancy in the Style of "Cul de Sac,"* mimicking Richard Thompson's 2004–12 comic strip; *Nancy's Aunt*, a drawing of Aunt Fritzi posed in the style of James McNeill Whistler's 1871 painting *Arrangement in Gray and Black Number 1*, better known as *Whistler's Mother*; and *Sailor Nancy*, which portrays Nancy as Sailor Moon. The idea that a strip's creator could make fan art of her own strip seems contradictory, but it also points to the difficulty of defining exactly what fan art is. Suzanne Scott broadly defines fan art as including "fan drawings and painting, as well as digital image manipulations, mashups, and even potentially animated GIFs."[31] However, she also notes that fan scholars have paid more attention to fanvids and fan fiction, so there has not been "a robust theorization of the practice" of fan art.[32] Jaimes's "fan art" might be taken in numerous ways. Much as Jaimes often questions her own talent in the strip, her ascription of "fan art" to her own work could be a means of playfully undermining her own authority as creator of the comic strip. Jaimes's "fan art" might also simply be her way of drawing *Nancy* in the style of other artists (such as she does in the Labor Day *Prince Valiant* strip). Creating fan art can be seen as a way of being #relatable. Jaimes's Nancy makes this point in a strip. On March 12, 2019, as they sit at a table, drawing, Agnes suggests that Nancy draw fan art. Nancy tells Agnes that she is "**already** drawing fan art" of herself as Thor and of Thor as herself. Each of Nancy's drawings is a stick figure drawing of herself holding a hammer. One is labeled "Thor," and one is labeled "Nancy." Nancy's attempt at relatability fails when Agnes cannot recognize that Nancy is creating fan art. This failure once again points to how Nancy is used by Jaimes as part of her persona and to how Jaimes voices ambivalence about being #relatable. Jaimes's *Nancy* fan art gestures toward *Nancy*'s material history as a legacy comic strip; in a sense, when she creates a new *Nancy* strip, she is making fan art. While a large part of Jaimes's persona is based in webcomics, her persona must also contend with both other artistic appropriations of Bushmiller's work by visual artists like Andy Warhol and Joe Brainard and with *Nancy*'s status as a legacy comic strip.

Working with Legacy Comics

In 1961 Andy Warhol included Nancy in his series of cartoon paintings that also included Dick Tracy and Popeye. As John Carlin notes in his overview of Nancy's use in art, Warhol's "fragmented and distressed" painting of Nancy made the image "work on a different, fine art scale," opening "the floodgates for a generation of artists to plunder the comics for their paintings' subjects."[33] Of all the artists who used comics, Joe Brainard made the most extensive use of Nancy. Like Jaimes's "fan art" that adapts *Nancy* to the style of famous painters, Joe Brainard's 1960s and 1970s appropriation of Bushmiller's work imagines Nancy as portrayed by various artists. Brainard's paintings include *Untitled (If Nancy Was a Drawing by Leonardo DaVinci)*, *Untitled (Nancy as a Goya)*, *If Nancy Was a Drawing by Larry Rivers*, *Picasso Nancy*, and three different works imagining Nancy as a work by Willem de Kooning.[34] While Jaimes uses her *Nancy* fan art to complicate her persona as *Nancy*'s creator, Brainard uses Nancy in multiple ways—he displays his admiration for Bushmiller, shows that he finds Nancy to be #relatable, and finds ways to experiment in his art. His appropriations show that Nancy has long been a character and icon open to reimagination.

Part of the reason why Joe Brainard used Nancy in his art was simply because, as Ann Lauterbach writes, his "favorite cartoon character was *Nancy*."[35] Ron Padgett, in his "The Origins of Joe Brainard's Nancy," tells us that "in his childhood Joe Brainard was well acquainted with Nancy, long before he started using her in his art," because his family subscribed to the *Tulsa Sunday World*, which included *Nancy* in its color comics section.[36] Padgett posits that Brainard's affinity for Nancy has roots in this childhood reading, which led to an appreciation of Bushmiller's style: "Joe admired Bushmiller's clean, bold line as his disposition of solid blacks against white . . . and . . . he enjoyed Bushmiller's agreeably dopey sense of humor."[37] Growing from this aesthetic appreciation, Brainard came to identify with Nancy. Padgett points out that Brainard's identification with Nancy "is far more complicated" than his admiration of Bushmiller's work.[38]

Lauterbach explores the multiple ways that Brainard identified with Nancy. She writes that Nancy, for Brainard, is everything from a "talisman" to a "transitional object" to a "distilled essence" to a "companion and guide."[39] Nancy's relatability underlies all these functions. If Brainard did not find Nancy #relatable, he would not have been able to put her character and image to such varied use. For Lauterbach, Brainard identified with Nancy's "apparent simplicity. . . . Like Joe, she appears to be without complexity, but in fact she often displays guile, resourcefulness, vanity, and appetite."[40] All the qualities that Olivia Jaimes uses to make Nancy #relatable—her ambition, her self-regard, her metaphorical and literal appetite—can be found in Bushmiller's legacy, and it is through these qualities that Brainard connects to Nancy. Lauterbach writes that as Brainard arrived in the New

York art world from his home in Tulsa, "Nancy . . . could be his virtual companion and side-kick" and be "inserted into this world, instantly stripping it of its formidable aura, transforming it into an accessible, intimate realm."[41] Through Nancy, Brainard could find "an accommodating, domestic nearness and here-ness" rooted in his childhood reading of the Sunday comics.[42]

Brainard would use Nancy's relatability to produce works of art that explored issues of "high" versus "low" art, representation and expression, and social constructions of sexuality. Lauterbach writes that in the mid-1960s, artists like Jasper Johns, Andy Warhol, and Roy Lichtenstein "had begun to map so-called 'low' elements, drawn from popular culture, into their works."[43] Brainard's use of Nancy—among other comic characters that he used in his art, such as Dick Tracy and L'il Abner—fit in with Warhol's paintings of Coke bottles, Campbell's soup cans, and Nancy and with Lichtenstein's appropriation of the visual language of comic strips. In addition, Lauterbach writes that Brainard uses Nancy "to experiment with color and form and to investigate ideas around subjectivity, perception, and the materiality of the object. [Nancy gives] Brainard a referential vocabulary of startling flexibility and range."[44] In short, Brainard used Nancy to create art investigating assumptions of what art could be and do.[45]

In paintings such as *Untitled (Nancy Descending a Staircase)* and *Untitled (Nancy in the Storm)*, Brainard inserts drawings of Nancy into reproductions of works by, respectively, Marcel Duchamp and Yves Tanguy. Lauterbach writes of these works, "This is Brainard at his most joyously subversive, defrocking the Holy Canon [of Western Art] while simultaneously inserting himself, via Nancy (and so the rest of us ordinary folks) into it."[46] Nancy serves here as a #relatable connection between the worlds of comic art and high art in Brainard's avant-garde work. Jaimes's fan art does not seem as invested in being subversive regarding distinctions between comics and other forms of art. Jaimes's Nancy can be in a Vermeer and in a *Cul de Sac* comic; her fan art is not interested in distinctions between levels of art. *Nancy*'s status as a legacy comic strip further complicates the material history of the strip and adds to the complex past that Jaimes must incorporate into her persona.

Legacy comic strips—or more unkindly, "zombie strips"—are comics that still exist after their creator has either died or quit the strip. Michael Cavna extends the metaphor of "zombie strip," writing that they "tend to linger long after their creators have died, taking to the grave too often the very inspiration for the strip itself. Still, these lifeless features take up newspaper space by finding new host bodies (often, this earthly duty falls to a relative, a spawn who dutifully draws the flat-line, if you will)."[47] For Cavna these strips would be better off fully dead. As I look at the comic page of my daily newspaper,[48] eight of the twenty-two comic strips are some variety of legacy strip, from the reruns of Charles Schulz's *Peanuts* and Lynne Johnston's *For Better or For Worse* to the corporate-written *Garfield* to the generationally continued *Family Circus* and *Dennis the Menace* to those strips passed on to new creators—*Rex Morgan*, *Judge Parker*, and *Blondie*. The idea that legacy strips are devoid of interest might in part account for why Charles Hatfield, in *Alternative Comics*, writes that daily newspaper comics are a relic of a previous age resistant to change.[49] While some legacy strips do seem to recycle the same old jokes again and again, many have been taken in new and interesting directions, like Karen Moy and June Brigman's *Mary Worth*; Peter Gallagher's *Heathcliff*; Jules Rivera's *Mark Trail*; and of course, Jaimes's *Nancy*. To dismiss all legacy strips as zombie strips is a mistake.

Legacy strips raise interesting questions about the ownership of characters. Schulz's *Peanuts*, while still being reprinted in many daily papers, is perhaps the most famous example of a strip ending with its creator's death, as Schulz's success gave him leverage to end his strip. The *Los Angeles Times* obituary for Schulz simply notes, "At the request of his five grown children, his syndicate contract stipulates that no other cartoonist draw it."[50] Schulz and his family felt that no cartoonist could add to the fifty-year legacy of *Peanuts*. While Schulz's contract has ensured that no new daily *Peanuts* comics have appeared since his death, the contract has not prevented the creation of new *Peanuts* content in other formats. BOOM! Entertainment has published a series of graphic novels and monthly comic books that mix together old Schulz *Peanuts* strips and new content to create what the studio calls "heartwarming tales . . . based on Charles M. Schulz's beloved PEANUTS Characters!"[51] In 2021 BOOM published "an original graphic novel" called *Peanuts: Scotland Bound, Charlie Brown* that is based on "an unproduced, feature-length special, storyboarded by Charles M. Schulz and Bill Melendez" that was found "in the archives of the Schulz Studio."[52] The 2015 computer-animated *The Peanuts Movie* was written by Schulz's son Craig Schulz and his grandson Bryan Schulz. In 2021 Apple TV premiered *The Snoopy Show*.

Schulz's contemporary, Ernie Bushmiller, exerted no control whatsoever over the characters in *Nancy*. As I will discuss in more detail in chapter 2, Ernie Bushmiller created Nancy as a minor character in the *Fritzi Ritz* comic strip. *Fritzi Ritz* was created in 1922 by Larry Whittington, and Bushmiller took over the strip in 1925 and introduced Fritzi's niece, Nancy, in 1935. The characters in *Fritzi Ritz* and *Nancy* have always been owned by the syndicate that published the strips. After Bushmiller's death on August 15, 1982, the strip continued, written by former Bushmiller apprentices. "*Nancy*, still a valuable property for United Features Syndicate, endured, after a fashion, continued initially by Will Johnson (dailies) and Al Plastino (Sundays), who had both worked under Bushmiller, and by a host of successors thereafter."[53] These writers, for the most part, followed Bushmiller's drawing and writing style, but Karasik and Newgarden write that the strip only "endured, after a fashion," as a pale imitation of its earlier years. The multiple creators assigned to *Nancy* over the years is a much more typical fate for a popular syndicated comic, in comparison to strips like *Peanuts* and *Calvin and Hobbes*, which both ended when their first and only creator stopped producing strips.

As Ian Gordon tells readers, questions of the ownership of comic characters have their roots in the origins of American newspaper comics in the 1890s, specifically in Richard Outcault's "Yellow Kid." Even as Outcault created a distinctive "individual character" in his *Hogan's Alley* comic, Gordon writes, "the Yellow Kid's meaning and reception often slipped from his creator's control."[54] Outcault failed to secure a copyright for the Yellow Kid's likeness and was thus unable to control the marketing of his creation. In turn, Outcault lost possible profits as "entrepreneurs marketed numerous unauthorized Yellow Kid products," including "songbooks . . . chewing gum . . . and ladies' fans."[55] Even as some comic creators were better paid in the early twentieth century than they are now, Outcault's desire to copyright the Yellow Kid shows that comic creators have always relied on merchandise sales as part of their income. Without a copyright on the character, when Outcault left the *New York World* for the *New York Journal* in 1896, he could not prevent the *World* from running George Luks's version of *Hogan's Alley*, which featured a "Yellow Kid" identical to Outcault's. Gordon writes, "The simultaneous appearance of two Yellow Kids in newspaper strips, and the flood of unlicensed products diminished the value of the character as a commodity for both Outcault and the publisher."[56] All the stakeholders lost potential profits, because the Yellow Kid was not anyone's property. Four years later, Outcault was able to copyright his newest character, Buster Brown, and he profited immensely from the marketing.[57] Yet when Outcault left the *New York Herald* for William Randolph Hearst's *New York American*, he lost the right to name his comic strip *Buster Brown*.

As *Nancy* became a legacy strip in the 1980s, the days when a creator could take their intellectual property to a competing newspaper syndicate were long gone. None of *Nancy*'s creators could lay claim to the strip's characters. United Features Syndicate could hire whomever they liked to create the strip. Comic creators in the twenty-first century rarely see the opportunity to sell their work to a higher bidder. Thus, *Nancy* continued on as one legacy strip among others. It was not until Guy Gilchrist took over the strip in 1995 that *Nancy* really changed, both in style and in content. Gilchrist made Nancy and Sluggo "cuter." They had more oval faces; they blushed, smiled, and cried and were more sentimental in expression and thought. Gilchrist's run of *Nancy* did not garner much critical attention, and when it ended in 2018, the strip went into limbo for a month and a half until the Andrews McMeel Syndicate's April 9, 2018, announcement that Jaimes would be taking over *Nancy*. Of course, like the strip's previous creators, Jaimes would not own any of *Nancy*'s characters; they are the intellectual property of Andrews McMeel Universal. Jaimes's notion that she is creating fan art of *Nancy* makes a certain amount of sense from this perspective, as the character is not hers. At the same time, one might be hard-pressed to consider *Nancy* as Jaimes's fan art, since Jaimes has been hired by the syndicate *as* the authorized creator of *Nancy*. This tension speaks to the ways that Jaimes has worked with *Nancy*'s history while making the strip contemporary. Jaimes's webcomic creator persona coexists and overlaps with her legacy comic creator persona.

Playing with *Nancy*'s Legacy

In her first month of creating *Nancy*, Jaimes addressed the strip's legacy. On April 30, readers see Nancy and Sluggo walking past some flowering bushes in a grassy area. Nancy says, "I'm sick of all these reboots and restarts." Nancy's legacy fans can read these lines as Nancy's metacommentary speaking to her own three-week-old reboot. As the strip continues, we see Nancy and Sluggo walking past bushes and flowers from which tiny black dots of pollen emanate. The gag is revealed by Sluggo's dialogue, "Look, I know you hate pollen but that's still a pretty harsh way to talk about spring." Nancy was talking about the changing of the seasons and the return of her spring allergies. She was not talking about her own reboot; of course, Jaimes is using Nancy as a mouthpiece to talk about her reboot of *Nancy*. Certainly, readers familiar with the history of *Nancy* were thinking about Jaimes's reboot. Many fans of Bushmiller's *Nancy* disdained Jaimes's reboot from its start,[58] and she seemed to anticipate some of this antipathy by referencing it before the fact, in the strip.

Separating the legacy and webcomic aspects of Jaimes's working persona is impossible. I understand them as part of Jaimes's flexibility as a comic creator. Paul Booth, in *Playing Fans: Negotiating Fandom and Media in the Digital Age*, argues that the boundaries between fans and media companies have blurred in recent years. He argues that fandom has become more "diffuse," with more media consumers identifying as fans and more media companies commodifying fan practices. He writes, "Both media fans and the media industries must continually negotiate, navigate, and adjust to the presence of each other in tandem with changing paradigms of technological discourse in our digital society."[59] Jaimes can portray herself as a media fan—she likes *Nancy*, creates fan art, and comments on *Nancy*'s history. At the same time, Jaimes is part of a media industry because of her job creating *Nancy*. Jaimes creates a space where she can both create new *Nancy* strips and comment on *Nancy*'s material legacy, as when Nancy asks on April 30, 2018, "Why can't something that's gone stay gone?" By opening this space, Jaimes is able to bring something novel to what might be considered merely nostalgic. Booth argues that "one important continuum that fans and the industry continue to navigate in their interactive relationship is that between nostalgia and novelty in digital fandom . . . fans continually look to iconic moments in a text's past to reference their fandom."[60] At the same time, fans seek novelty: "fresh material, new takes on old genres, and changing paradigms of meaning."[61] While Booth focuses mainly on television and digital fandom, what he writes applies easily to daily comic strips.

Jaimes's *Nancy*, like other flexible strips that appear both digitally and in print, inhabits an online space of constant feedback, anonymous commentary, and engaged reading. A brief look at any strip that appears on GoComics makes this obvious. Numerous familiar clickable icons appear to the right of every comic strip: a speech bubble, signifying "comment"; a heart, signifying "like"; a pin, to post on Pinterest; a lowercase *f*, to post a strip to Facebook; a bird, to post on Twitter; and ellipses to show "more sharing options." Each icon has a number under it, so readers can instantly know how many comments a strip has, how many times it has been liked, and so on. As Booth reminds fans, "Our clicks become capital. We are commoditized from and marketed to."[62] Our likes and links are calculated and fed into the kinds of algorithms that Sluggo mentions to Nancy (November 2, 2019). In fact, on March 22, 2019, Jaimes incorporates the look of web comment forms into the strip. In panel 1 we see Nancy lying on the floor while she draws a picture. In panel 2 we get a close-up of Nancy while

Sluggo says from outside panel, "Even if you post all the time, what really matters is whether or not you do well under the algorithm." Panel 3 pulls back to show Nancy and Sluggo sitting on the floor. Sluggo's words are repeated verbatim, as panel 3 gives us a wider view of the floor space. Sluggo looks at his phone as he speaks. Nancy is distracted from her drawing because a white rectangle takes up most of the space in the panel. The white rectangle contains four small boxes, each followed by a sentence: "Hide content like this," "I don't like content like this," "This content is not relevant," and "This content is spam." In other words, a typical online feedback form has infiltrated the diegetic space of the strip. In reaction to Sluggo's words, Nancy has checked the first two boxes and is in the process of checking the third. She is rejecting his advice even as she uses a form that proves the point of his advice. This joke clearly works better for digital readers, as the form in the panel almost looks like one more clickable option next to the extradiegetic icons that appear to the right of the strip.

Print readers of the strip might not even get the joke if they are not familiar with the workings of internet feedback. While this joke might not succeed in print, Jaimes must continually write for two audiences. Just as Jaimes's persona must encompass both her webcomic self and her legacy comic self, Jaimes's *Nancy* has to speak to print readers and digital readers. In one of her first Sunday strips (May 27, 2018), Jaimes addresses the literal media in which Nancy is read, as well as the generational shifts that one's choice of medium might mark. A large first panel has a text box that says, "Humor is always changing." We see three versions of Nancy: first, a black-and-white Nancy reads a large Sunday comic section; second, a muted but in-color Nancy reads a comic book; third, a full-color Nancy reads on her phone screen. All three Nancys are laughing as they read. The second panel's text box reads, "Something that is baffling to one generation might be hilarious to another." The third panel shows Nancy reading *Nancy* on a computer screen. Readers can see the screen—it is a miniature version of the whole strip—that is, the laptop screen shows all four panels of that day's strip, illustrating that *Nancy* is legible in print and on screens. Jaimes's dual audience can be considered as more than just a question of the medium through which readers consume *Nancy*, though. This strip makes visible the competing aspects of relatability. As a legacy comic creator, Jaimes must address long-standing fans of Ernie Bushmiller's *Nancy*. These fans can roughly equate to those whom Booth sees as seeking nostalgia in their reading experience. Jaimes's *Nancy* must also speak to fans who seek novelty and have little awareness of the strip's history. Other readers might share aspects of the nostalgic fan or the novelty seeker. Jules Rivera has confronted this same issue in her recent reimagining of *Mark Trail*. Unlike Jaimes, who does not directly engage with readers, Rivera directly confronts and makes fun of nostalgic fans on Twitter. On November 18, 2020, she posted a screen capture of someone telling her, "You are RUINING Mark Trail." Rivera's response to this critic was immediate: "Dudes be sliding into my DMs begging me to give it up."[63] If readers can respond to a strip the moment it is published, Rivera shows that creators can respond to readers just as quickly. While Jaimes never directly engages with fans online, about the strip's legacy or anything else, she does speak to fans about *Nancy*'s legacy within the strip.

I discuss above how Jaimes has continued Bushmiller's tradition of Labor Day strips about the work of a comic creator. She has also carried on Bushmiller's tradition of publishing April Fool's jokes on April 1. Bushmiller preferred absurdist jokes. In one, Nancy is drawn out of proportion in the first three panels, and the off-panel cartoonist proclaims, "April Fool" in the final panel (April 1, 1946). In others, Nancy walks on the wall and ceiling (April 1, 1947), and Nancy and Sluggo switch heads (April 1, 1948). Jaimes employs a different April Fool's strategy. In the April 1 strip from both 2019 and 2020, Jaimes directly addresses readers regarding some aspect of *Nancy*'s legacy. In 2020 Jaimes constructs the strip as an "F.A.Q. about Nancy, with Olivia Jaimes." The first question is "Why hasn't Nancy aged over the strip's eighty-year run?" Jaimes answers that Nancy is a vampire. Instead of answering the next two questions about where Nancy lives and why her hair has spikes, Jaimes continues the joke that Nancy is a vampire. Jaimes portrays herself as an expert on *Nancy*'s history. She does the same on April 1, 2019, but with a joke more firmly based in an aspect of Bushmiller's *Nancy*. In a direct address to readers in the top third of the first panel, Jaimes writes, "Die-hard fans of *Nancy* will recall that original artist and creator, Ernie Bushmiller, nearly always drew rocks in precise groups of three." In the bottom third of the panel, we see a typical Bushmiller-style drawing of three rocks. Careful readers of Jaimes's *Nancy* may have noticed that Jaimes had rarely drawn rocks in the strip and never in a grouping of three. This absence of rocks can be read as a nearly yearlong setup for this April Fool's joke. In panel 2 Jaimes explains that "as all true fans know, he developed this habit during World War II," as wartime shortages limited the number of rocks cartoonists could draw. Under the text box is a pamphlet called "Three Is Enough!" The third panel includes a "rejected" Bushmiller cartoon from 1966, in which Nancy hides a bottle of cod liver oil from Aunt Fritzi under "this fourth rock." Jaimes, the expert, tells us, "What some might not know is that later in his career, Bushmiller attempted to experiment with higher numbers of rocks, only to be swiftly shut down by his editors." Panel 4 provides the true gag, as Jaimes writes, "I'm humbled to make his true vision . . . a reality." We see Nancy (on a hoverboard, as she is in the Labor Day 2019 strip) on a sidewalk and grassy area covered by at least thirty-two rocks. Jaimes shows readers that she understands Bushmiller's legacy, and she refers to it just often enough to remind readers of her knowledge. In claiming to present Bushmiller's "true vision of *Nancy*," Jaimes embraces her role as the keeper of his legacy (even as she undermines this embrace as an April Fool's joke).

Jaimes's *Nancy* shares many recurring motifs with Bushmiller's *Nancy* (and with many daily comic strips focused on children, from *Peanuts* to *Big Nate*): attempts to hide bad report cards, despair at the beginning of the school year, complaints about studying and chores, tricks to sneak dessert, lying in bed at night worrying, and anticipating holidays (especially Halloween and Christmas). As I will discuss in chapter 3, Jaimes also uses comic strip humor that was codified by Bushmiller and others in the early and mid-twentieth century, from absurdism and visual and textual puns to tricks with perspective, lines of sight, motion lines, and gutters. But perhaps the strongest legacy aspect of Jaimes's *Nancy* has to do with Nancy's personality.

Nancy's grouchiness has long been her defining characteristic. When Jaimes was planning the first strips for her reboot, she read some of Guy Gilchrist's *Nancy* run. For Jaimes, with Gilchrist at the helm, "Nancy as a character had drifted from where I envision her. . . . And I was like, *I need to do a character-reset week*."[64] Gilchrist's sweet, lovable Nancy, who even sported a pink bow at times instead of her traditional red one, had become saccharine. Jaimes's "character-reset week" was, among other things, a return to the smart-aleck, snarky, scheming, mean, and always hungry Nancy of Bushmiller's day. Jaimes's statement, from the press release announcing her reboot of *Nancy*, bears repeating: "Nancy has been my favorite sassy grouch for a long time."[65] Above, I argue that Jaimes uses this statement to connect her own persona to Nancy's. Jaimes's declaration also shows that Nancy's grouchiness itself has a history. Before her strip even appears, Jaimes says that Bushmiller's creation of Nancy's personality is a key aspect of the character's legacy and one that Jaimes would be relying on. I do not mean to suggest that Jaimes simply takes Nancy's ready-made attitude from Bushmiller. Instead, I mean that while Nancy has been a "sassy grouch" for much of her run, a 1940s sassy grouch is radically different from a 2020s sassy grouch. As I discuss in the next chapter, mid-twentieth-century Nancy was a grouch because adults were mean to her, because she was ashamed of her bodily appearance, and because she was romantically interested in, and jealous of, Sluggo. Twenty-first-century Nancy is a sassy grouch because she works to be famous and to achieve at school as she navigates friendship and difference through social media. Nancy's personality signifies differently in 2018 than it did in 1948. The Nancy of 2018 lives much of her life online. As a character, she now shapes her personality through blogging, posting pictures, and joining group chats. In the next chapter, I will focus on how Jaimes's relationship with *Nancy*'s online fan community works as a kind of real-world reflection of Nancy the character's social media relationships. Jaimes uses *Nancy*, the comic strip, to establish the changing representational practices of contemporary flexible comics. She uses Nancy, the character, to make these practices part of the content of the strip. As Jaimes adapts the strip to the twenty-first century, *Nancy* becomes #relatable in new ways.

3. *Nancy*, by Olivia Jaimes, June 4, 2018. NANCY © 2018. Reprinted by permission of ANDREWS MCMEEL SYNDICATION for UFS. All rights reserved.

2

"New Year, New Me!"

Nancy's Representations (June 4, 2018)

Old and New Fritzi

Jaimes's *Nancy* debuted on April 9, 2018. Nancy's aunt Fritzi does not speak on panel in the strip until June 4.[1] Her first words are "New year, new me!" Nancy quickly points out, "The new year started months ago." Nonetheless, Fritzi continues her proclamation in the next two panels as Nancy continues to note the illogic of Fritzi's claims. The positioning of Nancy and Fritzi as they converse is quite strange. In each panel, they stand next to each other but do not look at each other. They seem to be looking forward, at a space outside the strip (at least until Fritzi turns her eyes toward Nancy in the final panel). As Karin Kukkonen explains in *Studying Comics and Graphic Novels*, a character's "deictic gaze" shows us what a character is looking at and draws our own eyes toward what the character sees. A deictic gaze is "a gaze that shows you something."[2] Knowing what a character is looking at can tell a reader a lot about what is going on in a strip. When Fritzi turns her gaze toward Nancy in panel 3, readers can tell that she is annoyed with Nancy's smart-aleck commentary. Before this turn, though, both Nancy and Fritzi appear to be looking toward the reader, even as they talk to each other. Their gaze, then, suggests a certain meta quality to this strip—Nancy and Fritzi are talking to *Nancy*'s readers. In looking outward, they reinforce the #relatable quality of the strip as they subtly tell readers that a change is coming. This conversation with readers sets up the series of strips that focus on Fritzi's new look.

Most of the strips that deal with Fritzi's "new me" share this quality of gesturing toward readers. In the days after the June 4, 2018, strip, Fritzi gives away all her old clothes, so that according to Nancy, on June 7, 2018, "all she has left are exercise clothes." Subsequently, Fritzi wears jeans and plain T-shirts or relatively loosely shaped one-color dresses. Jaimes's redesign of Fritzi reaches a sort of satiric high point in the "Sluggo is lit" Labor Day strip of September 3, 2018.[3] One of the fake future panels in this strip shows Fritzi in very puffy overalls saying, ". . . And that's why I'm only wearing snowsuits from now on!" The final panel of this strip shows Fritzi wearing an incredibly bulky hooded snowsuit. She is indoors, wearing slippers, and serving a plate of food to Nancy. New *Nancy* readers might be confused at this point, as Jaimes has never shown us the older version of Fritzi. But Jaimes and nostalgic readers of *Nancy* are familiar with Fritzi's legacy. Making Fritzi new led Jaimes to consider how different kinds of readers relate to the character.

In a discussion of the Labor Day 2018 strip, Jaimes describes how she came up with the imaginary future panels: "And then I was like, actually, what are the panels that would most upset the person who likes me the least? The most upsetting panel to someone who's like, 'Nancy sucks now'?"[4] As I mention in my introduction, Jaimes has a "protective policy" of not reading online comments about *Nancy*. Instead, she consulted her editor for advice. Jaimes continues, "I was joking with her at the very beginning about how I was going to make Fritzi wear a parka, and she was like 'People would hate that.'"[5] So Jaimes establishes a distance from her fans, shielded by her editor, but she engages with them, "replying" to fans in actual strips rather than in online forums or comment sections. In short, when Jaimes redesigned Fritzi, she anticipated readers' reactions to this redesign and addressed it in the strip, both in the deictic gaze of June 4 and in the exaggeration of September 3. Before discussing the exact aspects of Fritzi that Jaimes has changed from *Nancy*'s legacy, I want to make a claim about the importance of this redesign. The new Fritzi serves as an index of the new representations of gender and race that Jaimes brings to the strip. These representations confront the sexist and racist histories that are part not just of *Nancy* but also of legacy strips in general. Jaimes's redesign of Fritzi, along with her introduction of a multiracial and primarily female cast of new characters, alters the ways that identity works in twenty-first-century flexible daily comics. These different identities, in turn, lead to different ways of relating to *Nancy*.

Jaimes's status as the first female creator of *Nancy* plays a large role in how readers have responded to her work. Fan communities can easily become toxic and threatening, especially toward female fans and creators. Suzanne Scott's *Fake Geek Girls: Fandom, Gender, and the Convergence Culture Industry* details "the proliferation of misogyny within contemporary geek culture."[6] Scott's focus on "geek culture" encompasses a wide landscape of television, cinema, and comic book fandoms, among others. These fandoms form a large part of the culture industry surrounding media properties, spanning not only discussion forums but also fan-created and fan-tailored fiction, art, movies, and fashion. A lot of money is at stake in the ways that the culture industry interacts with fans. Daily comic strip fandom is dwarfed in size by those larger fandoms and is a lower-stakes affair, taking place in the comments section of GoComics and Comics Kingdom and in Facebook groups; there is no *Nancy* Cinematic Universe. Nonetheless, the misogyny that Scott traces through larger fandoms certainly exists in the much smaller space of *Nancy* fandom.

Nancy has spawned numerous Facebook groups, including the Fritzi Ritz Appreciation Society (176 members), It's the FRITZI RITZ Group (4,700 members), Friends of (Ernie Bushmiller's) Sluggo (2,900 members), the Bizarro Nancy Critics Society (507 members), the *How to Read "Nancy"* Reading Group (5,000 members), and *Nancy* by Olivia Jaimes Reading Group (53 members). One does not have to read far into these online spaces to understand why Jaimes does not read the comments. The "About" page for the Bizarro Nancy Critics Society states that the group is "for critical discussion of the comic strip travesty currently masquerading as the beloved 'Nancy.'" The vast majority of discussion in these groups is civil and seriously invested in closely reading *Nancy*, but most of these groups favor Ernie Bushmiller's *Nancy* and are nostalgic and male dominated. The *How to Read "Nancy"* Reading Group takes its name from Karasik and Newgarden's book about Bushmiller's *Nancy*. That group shares much overlap with the "Bizarro" group, which takes its name from a time when Bushmiller's work was being revalued by a contingent of comic writers and avant-garde artists. This trend continues in some ways, especially online. Comic creator and critic Scott McCloud wrote, "Ernie Bushmiller's comic strip *Nancy* is a landmark achievement: A comic so simply drawn it can be reduced to the size of a postage stamp and still be legible."[7] Hillary Chute notes that Bushmiller's *Nancy* is a favorite of cartoonists like Art Spiegelman and Chris Ware and has been "redrawn by [Gary] Panter . . . as well as by Charles Burns, Ivan Brunetti, and many, many others."[8] Chute pinpoints what most of these creators value in Bushmiller's *Nancy* when she cites Gary Panter, who tells a critic that Bushmiller's comic "functions as a nostalgic buffer against future shock for a tired and technology-torn species."[9] This thought, combined with Karasik and Newgarden's idea that "if we are making comics and cannot *think* like Bushmiller, there is little hope,"[10] shows how much these readers venerate Bushmiller. In this view, Bushmiller—the hardworking, brilliantly successful writer of comic strip gags—stands as a big part of *Nancy*'s legacy that Jaimes has to engage with in her reboot of the strip.

Bill Griffith, creator of the daily comic *Zippy the Pinhead*, has written that "*Nancy* tells us what it's like to be a comic strip."[11] Nancy, Sluggo, and even the more obscure Phil Fumble have made appearances in numerous *Zippy* strips over the years, making Griffith the comic creator with perhaps the most engaged, detailed connection to Bushmiller's work. In *Zippy* Griffith has delineated what makes *Nancy* work as a comic strip. His exploration of Bushmiller's humor is exemplified by a long strip called "It's Bushmiller Time," in which Zippy "subconsciously saunters into the elegant essence of Cartoon Reality" and pops in on Ernie Bushmiller.[12] Zippy asks, "What is fun, Ernie?" and Ernie succinctly answers, "Three Rocks."[13] Zippy asks a series of questions and is refuted each time. "Four rocks?" "No—" "Two rocks?" "Sorry—" "One rock?" "No— three rocks." Zippy then sits on a grouping of three rocks and contemplates their funness, when Nancy herself shows up, picks up the three rocks as one unit, and says, "Give me those things—I need them for a gag."[14] Griffith's focus on the comedic aspect of three rocks prefigures Jaimes's April 1, 2019, strip on the subject (as discussed in chapter 1). The absence of three rocks in the first year of Jaimes's strip is clearly an homage to Bushmiller's strip and to die-hard fans like Griffith.

Griffith coins the term "Bushmillerland" to describe what he sees as the timeless aspect of the strip.[15] In his introduction to the collection of Bushmiller strips *Nancy Loves Sluggo*, cartoonist and critic Ivan Brunetti makes a similar point. He writes that in *Nancy* "there spans a whole universe of drawing, an inexhaustible system of depicting reality . . . the linear clarity of a Platonic substructure that maps our existence in the world."[16] In short, Bushmiller wields tremendous influence in certain parts of comic culture. It is worth noting that most of these fans of Bushmiller are male; the title of a *New York Review of Books* essay about *How to Read "Nancy"* sums up this point nicely: "Grown Men Reading 'Nancy.'"[17] The overwhelming maleness of Bushmiller fandom makes Jaimes's status as the first woman to write and draw *Nancy* especially interesting. The *How to Read "Nancy"* Reading Group has an oft-repeated rule: "When in doubt—KEEP IT ERNIE!" This rule gets cited when discussion of Jaimes's *Nancy* occurs, as it sometimes does. For instance, during a November 27, 2018, discussion of an interview with Jaimes that was published online, a member of the group responded to what they saw as the sexist vitriol being directed at Jaimes. They wrote, "This feels a bit like a dudes hatin fest in here." This poster's characterization of the discussion—that male fans were criticizing Jaimes because of her gender—was challenged by other posters until the debate was brought to an end by moderators.

The group's directive to "keep it Ernie" succinctly summarizes the attitude of nostalgic fans of *Nancy*'s legacy. On April 24, 2018, a few weeks after Jaimes's reboot premiered, a commenter in the *How to Read "Nancy"* Reading Group crystalized the view of nostalgic *Nancy* fans. After reading Jaimes's strip, the commenter wrote, "What bothers me about the update is . . . why? [. . .] It's appealing to a generation who probably does not know who Nancy is." Asking why the strip needs to be updated implies that Bushmiller's *Nancy* should be left alone as an unchanging relic of the past. The commenter's point that fans of the new *Nancy* are a "generation" unaware of *Nancy*'s history once again highlights the multiple audiences that legacy comic creators must relate to. While this commenter claims that they cannot relate to the new *Nancy*, Jaimes seems to say that she sees nostalgic fans as a group that can relate to the new *Nancy*. Jaimes's April 30, 2018, strip, in which Nancy asks, "Why can't something that's gone stay gone?" anticipates the nostalgic fan's reaction.[18] In effect, Jaimes is saying to the nostalgic fan, "I can relate to your desire for my strip to not exist."

To return to Jaimes's redesign of Fritzi, I want to note that these nostalgic fan groups serve, in part, as self-appointed keepers of what they see as *Nancy*'s legacy. A brief history of Fritzi's character can illustrate this point. Fritzi Ritz was created by Larry Whittington in 1922 for his *Fritzi Ritz* comic strip. Ernie Bushmiller took over the strip in 1925 and created the character of Nancy in 1935. Nancy's popularity over the next few years led to the strip being renamed *Nancy* in 1938. Whittington, and then Bushmiller, drew Fritzi like a pinup model. She posed in a bathing suit or in high heels and slim-fitting skirts and blouses. Her boyfriend and other men in the strip ogled her, and many of the strip's gags involved men distracted by Fritzi's body. Guy Gilchrist altered the appearance of Aunt Fritzi in the 1990s. He abandoned her 1920s-style sexuality; instead, he drew Fritzi wearing tight, cleavage-baring T-shirts. In short, as Karasik and Newgarden write, "Fritzi Ritz sold gags—but Fritzi Ritz also sold sex."[19] They go on to note that Bushmiller's wife, Abby, "the slender, stylish daughter of a Bronx El train conductor," was an "occasional Fritzi model."[20] As Bob Kennedy wrote in *Hogan's Magazine: The Online Magazine of the Cartoon Arts*, "The funny pages have had their share of torchy sirens over the past century. Fritzi Ritz, Brenda Starr [and others] have inspired many a hormonally charged young lad to try his hand at drawing."[21] Tom Heintjes has noted that characters such as Fritzi were "rooted firmly in the idioms of the era. Flapper humor was one of the pop-art signatures of the Jazz Age, and strips showcasing attractive ditzes—notably, written by men working in an industry almost completely bereft of women—were commonplace, from Cliff Sterrett's *Polly and Her Pals* to Chic Young's *Dumb Dora* to Edgar Martin's *Boots and Her Buddies* to John Held Jr.'s *Merely Margy*."[22] In fact, Whittington was hired away by William Randolph Hearst to write the *Fritzi Ritz* clone strip *Maizie the Model* for King Features.[23] In short, then, Fritzi Ritz is a sex symbol from another era whose character remained largely unchanged for seventy years. Nostalgic comic fans have not forgotten this, as Jaimes knows.

In not reading comments and in preemptively "replying" to fans through the strip and via her editor's filter, Jaimes avoids the hatred that runs through internet commentary, while she creates strips that mean different things to different audiences, from the die-hard legacy readers to the novelty-seeking newer fans. Jaimes's strategy of fan engagement works for her and the strip. Other creators cultivate a different relationship with readers. As mentioned in chapter 1, Jules Rivera directly engages and makes fun of nostalgic *Mark Trail* fans. Unlike Jaimes, Rivera clearly reads the comments surrounding her strip. Like Jaimes, though, Rivera has introduced newer technologies into her strip. Mark Trail, who in previous iterations of the strip was a features writer for a nature magazine, has accepted a freelance job working for *Teen Girl Sparkle*. As part of his new job, he films nature videos that are posted online. In the March 17, 2021, strip, Mark makes a video about crickets in which he says, "Crickets are land shrimp." A few days later, Mark's editor at *Teen Girl Sparkle* informs him that the video has gone viral on BikBok (the strip's version of TikTok) because it has been sampled by an "eco rapper." On March 25 she tells him, "This is a golden opportunity to build your brand." As noted earlier, Rivera interacts with fans online, tweeting about Mark Trail cosplayers who have posted pictures online and noting that "teenage girls [are] shipping Mark with a peacock."[24] Mark Trail going viral in the strip mirrors the way that the strip itself has had viral moments. Even as she connects with *Mark Trail*'s newer online audience, Rivera also relates to nostalgic Mark Trail fans. The "Crickets are land shrimp" line is a callback to a monthslong 2016 series of *Mark Trail* created by James Allen where Mark is trapped in a cave. In September 2016 Mark tells Carina, who is trapped with him, that cave crickets are edible and that "some people call them 'land shrimp.'" This kind of interacting with fans is part of the job for webcomic creators, but such interactions can become dangerous. Sarah Andersen, creator of *Sarah's Scribbles*, tells an interviewer that "I always spend some time reading comments after the comic goes live to see how people are responding."[25] When asked for "advice on how to engage your followers," Andersen recommends keeping some distance, because fans "should get to know you through your work." She also warns against taking negative feedback as fans "attacking you as person," while also noting that she is "lucky to have never dealt with serious harassment or trolls (knock on wood). . . . But harassment does happen." Likewise, Sean Kleefeld notes in *Webcomics* that creators can be subject to "hate speech" meant to silence their voices.[26] He tells readers that Sophie Labelle, creator of the webcomic *Assigned Male*, which "is aimed . . . at the transgender community," has "had to cancel personal appearances and relocate entirely after being on the receiving end of death threats."[27] Jaimes's pseudonymity protects her from such personal attacks. She also short-circuits hateful commentary about her redesign of the sexy Aunt Fritzi by addressing possible objections to the redesign within the strip itself.

It is worth reiterating here that Jaimes's strip, while it certainly pays attention to *Nancy*'s legacy, *is* something new. Her recreation of Aunt Fritzi from a 1920s Jazz Age idealized beauty to a contemporary woman whose job seems to entail staring at a computer screen illustrates how Jaimes's strip represents a certain kind of twenty-first-century subjectivity, especially in relation to gender and racial identity. In her reconfiguration of Nancy's friend group and of the strip's secondary characters, Jaimes shows how gender and race signify differently in twenty-first-century comics, especially in relation to legacy comic strips of the twentieth century.

If Fritzi Ritz was once used to sell sex, her desire for a "new me" should make readers think about her differently. As mentioned in my introduction, new materialism often focuses on the roles that objects play in wider fields of social negotiations. Diana Coole and Samantha Frost write about how objects, bodies, and subjectivities connect to each other within larger social systems. For them, it is worth paying serious attention to "objects forming and emerging within relational fields, bodies composing their natural environment in ways that are corporeally meaningful for them, and subjectivities being constituted as open series of capacities or potencies . . . within a multitude of organic and social processes."[28] Fritzi's new clothes, through interaction with her body, form a new subjectivity for her character. If Fritzi is no longer an object to be ogled, her new identity remains somewhat ambiguous. Readers simply do not know much about Fritzi. Her job is never defined, and her relationships with other adults rarely get attention. We are never even told why Nancy lives with her; Nancy's parents are never mentioned. Fritzi's role as loving caretaker of Nancy serves to define her. At the same time, Fritzi's subjectivity seems quite similar to other characters. She struggles to avoid spending all her time online; she talks to Nancy about friendship and responsibility. Fritzi is a part of the cast of the strip, rather than an outsized adult force whose main purpose is to punish Nancy when she misbehaves (her usual role in Bushmiller's strip). Fritzi shares with Nancy and the rest of the cast a concern about how to live in a technologically mediated world. Jaimes has called Fritzi "a self-insert" and said that she identifies more with Fritzi than with Nancy, "because I feel bad if I step on people's toes."[29] Essentially, Fritzi is an adult version of Nancy, calmer and more evenhanded. Jaimes even makes fun of her rebooted Fritzi on January 7, 2019, when Nancy excitedly tells Fritzi that the characters in her favorite video game "are getting **new outfits**" as part of a "special event." Fritzi thinks to herself, "That's it? New clothes? Only the laziest creator would make a special event out of that." Fritzi then notes that she is shopping for new clothes for her and Nancy to wear next week "in an exclusive limited run." Jaimes also seems to be referring to her own redesign of Fritzi from a few months earlier. Nonetheless, Fritzi's new clothes serve as a marker of her new identity and of multiple other new identities in the strip.

In "Reading Spaces," Katherine Kelp-Stebbins argues that how we read comics is always historically contingent, grounded in cultural ideologies and societal norms. For Kelp-Stebbins, ignoring these contingencies can lead to an ahistorical formalism that sees no connection between the techniques used by comics (including everything from page layout to how comics signify movement through time) and the ways that the cultures surrounding comics shape and, in turn, are shaped by these formalist techniques. Kelp-Stebbins writes that readers must consider "what types of operations and distinctions comics articulate and, in turn, how users—both artists and readers alike—activate and mobilize these technical possibilities into emergent forms of expression and meaning."[30] Readers, creators, print and digital technologies, and formal conventions work together, enmeshed in each other both consciously and unconsciously, to create and illustrate new ways of being in the world. The material conditions of the world shape and are shaped by comics in ordinary and extraordinary ways. Something as basic as the medium of presentation can enable different kinds of representations. Kelp-Stebbins writes, "The patterns of signification that occur in a daily newspaper strip published in the late twentieth century in the United States will diverge in relevant ways from those of a page in a graphic novel such as *Persepolis* circulating through a number of geographically imbricated print economies in the twenty-first century."[31] Importantly, in this configuration, these divergent "patterns of signification" are not part of a hierarchy. A graphic novel does not hold more potential for signification than a daily comic strip. Rather, both hold potential to shape and be shaped by cultural and socioeconomic forces. As Kelp-Stebbins writes, "Such regimes necessarily frame a political sensibility and play a role in the formation of certain reading communities in space and time."[32] So for example, Olivia Jaimes's readers might focus on the nostalgic or the new; they might situate Jaimes as part of a comics tradition or read her work as a comment on identity or technology. They may read her strips in a print newspaper, on a phone or computer screen, or collected in a book. They may be compelled to comment online, or they may forget the strip the moment their eyes leave it. Meaning gets created through and in the interaction of creator, reader, and reading technology in specific times and spaces. Relatability gets constantly renegotiated. I will return in chapter 3 to the role that technology plays in making meaning in *Nancy*; for now, I want to focus on a neglected point of comic history to think more about how *Nancy*'s legacy might help to shape the ways readers think about emergent identities in contemporary comics.

Girlfriends

Michelle Ann Abate, in *Funny Girls*, provides an important historical context that might inform the way contemporary readers think about Jaimes's *Nancy*. Abate shows that Nancy is one among many preadolescent girls in comic strips and comic books, along with Little Lulu, Little Orphan Annie, and others, who seem to have been forgotten in or erased from the history of golden age comics in the first half of the twentieth century. Abate writes, "Many of the earliest, most successful, and most influential comics in the United States during this era featured young female protagonists."[33] Abate's work is not just a recuperation of these characters. She shows that these girl characters were "part of a larger cultural phenomenon" involved in "questioning traditional gender roles."[34] In addition, Abate argues that "these strips offer compelling and heretofore overlooked insights about major sociopolitical issues such as the societal perceptions of children, popular representations of girlhood, and changing national attitudes regarding youth and youth culture."[35] Reading these comics, including, of course, Bushmiller's *Nancy*, can shed light on how children interacted with adults, how social class coded feminine and masculine behavior, what kinds of work- and school-related stresses girls faced, and what romantic expectations were held for them during this time period. In other words, girl-centered comics of the early and mid-twentieth century played a role in both forming and questioning legible subjectivities.

Jaimes's twenty-first-century *Nancy*, then, confronts and alters much of *Nancy*'s early and mid-twentieth-century legacy. Ernie Bushmiller often focused on economic class in a way befitting the strip's emergence just before and during the Depression era. Sluggo had a strong Bronx accent, using words like "boid" for *bird* and "toikey" for *turkey*. This accent served as one of several markers of his poverty. He lived in a broken-down house with holes in the ceiling and trash in the yard, and his clothes were threadbare. Bushmiller's *Nancy* was also populated with secondary characters who personified the markers of social and economic class. Poor kids wore ragged clothes and spoke with accents, while rich kids lived in mansions, dressed neatly, and even had names like "Rollo the Rich Kid." Rich men walked Bushmiller's streets in top hats and waistcoats.

While Sluggo and Nancy have always been eight or nine years old, Bushmiller portrayed their relationship as romantic in a way that might have seemed perfectly rational to 1940s readers but might strike contemporary readers as strange or even creepy. In Sluggo's first appearance in *Nancy*, he protects her from a bully and then says, "Wanna be my goil?" (January 24, 1938). Both Nancy and Sluggo often thought of their future as a married couple, exemplified by the shop-window wedding cakes that feature prominently in Bushmiller's strip. Bushmiller often drew sexualized girls as foils to Nancy and Sluggo's boyfriend-girlfriend relationship. These girls inspired Sluggo's amorous attention and Nancy's jealousy. Nancy referred collectively to these children as "blonde vamps" and often considered herself homely in comparison to them.

Jaimes's representations of gender work quite differently from Bushmiller's for many reasons, including their respective social and economic contexts. The fact that Jaimes has a long legacy to contend with comes into play, too, as many of her decisions about characters might seem to be, at least in part, a response to the strip's past. In discussing her vision for the characters, Jaimes notes with relief that her editor told her, "Just so you know, you don't have to have Sluggo keep his accent."[36] Jaimes also notes the strangeness of Sluggo's preadolescent libido in legacy strips: "Classic Sluggo also was kinda doing the thing where he's like, 'Yowza, what a pretty girl!' Like, 'Bow wow!' And they're 8 years old."[37] In Bushmiller's strips, Sluggo's roving eye often prompted jealousy on Nancy's part, but Jaimes has written only one of these sexual jealousy strips. On April 24, 2018, readers see Nancy looking out from a window of her house as Sluggo talks to an unnamed girl. She says, "I wish Sluggo wouldn't talk to other girls." She continues in panel 2,

"If only I knew what they were talking about." Whereas "classic" Sluggo might have complimented the girl's appearance or asked her to go steady, here he is impressed because the girl's parents "have accounts for HBO and Hulu." Desire for technology replaces desire for romance. This girl never appears again in *Nancy*, and Jaimes has noted that while "Nancy's not gonna become nice . . . maybe she can lay off Sluggo if he talks to other girls."[38] This is indeed what happens. Nancy and Sluggo are friends, and Jaimes's strip spends much more time exploring Nancy's friendships with other girls than at any point in the strip's history.

Character development can be difficult to include in a daily comic strip, because time does not move forward in any normal way in most strips. Characters usually do not age; instead they mark the same milestones year after year: the beginning and end of the school year, summer vacation, holidays, the changing of the seasons. Along with Frank King's *Gasoline Alley*, Lynne Johnston's *For Better or For Worse* is one of the few daily comic strips that aged its characters, and even that strip did not age its characters consistently. Johnston notes, "I allowed the characters to age annually. This has made for some questions about actual dates and ages, when they don't line up perfectly."[39] Indeed, if Nancy had aged with the strip, she would be nearly one hundred years old. Even with her characters' unchanging ages, Jaimes has sought ways to have the characters change. She says, "I think of them maybe having some kind of development in some way. She doesn't grow up; like, doesn't turn 10 or go to college or anything. But she can learn something and have some kind of story line."[40] Jaimes's major story lines so far have focused on Nancy's relationship with her best friend Esther.

Nancy and Esther meet when they both join the robotics club. On May 22, 2018, they have their first conversation about how they both hate the club. After they try to one up each other on their indifference, the final panel shows them sharing a thought bubble: "Must . . . be the one . . . who cares the least . . ." A few days later, Esther asks Nancy, "Should we exchange usernames?" (May 26, 2018). Their technology-mediated friendship begins in earnest in the next panel, when Esther thinks that Nancy's social media will give her "my first real sense of who she is as a person." The final panel shows a close up of Esther's phone on Nancee22's Instagram-like page, where she sees nine photos of ice cream. Months later, Esther gets mad at Nancy and tells her, "I don't want to just be your stand-in for Sluggo" (September 20, 2018). Nancy promises to be a better friend. Nancy and Esther's friendship functions as another #relatable aspect of the strip as it is grounded in the material reality of the twenty-first century. Most obviously, as we see them texting back and forth and closely reading each other's social media feeds, it is clear that their friendship is technologically mediated. More subtly, their friendship connects to our sociopolitical times, parallel-ing Abate's argument that early and mid-twentieth-century girl comic characters are grounded in their times. Nancy and Esther's friendship reflects what Akane Kanai calls "shared attachments to managing imperfections."[41] The two girls sit next to each other in school, and Jaimes often presents them as conspiring together to take shortcuts with schoolwork or as not paying attention in class. On May 31, 2018, Esther and Nancy sit at a table with a laptop on it. Their teacher asks them how they are doing on a group project. Esther replies, "I'm really impressed with Nancy." In the final panel, we see why: "I've never seen someone minimize a screen so **fast**." A few weeks later their teacher asks them if they're making progress on an assigned math problem. Nancy replies, "We're making progress on **a** math problem" (June 19, 2018). The final panel shows a piece of paper on which the girls are calculating the "number of seconds left in school."

Nancy and Esther continue to bond as they prepare for the robotics club tournament. Eventually, Nancy skips practice to stay home and play video games, and her teacher removes her from the team (January 28, 2019). The team loses in the tournament, and Nancy and Esther's friendship is damaged. On January 30, 2019, Nancy wonders how mad her teammates are. A panel shows a close-up of Esther scowling at Nancy. After the team loses, Esther tells Nancy, "You only ever think of yourself! You hurt the people around you by being selfish!" (February 8, 2019). For months after this, Esther remains mad at Nancy. They only talk briefly at school, and Nancy cannot bring herself to apologize. The story line about their friendship breaking up continues until July 16, 2019, when they make up. Other story lines and unrelated strips occur during this time, but for a daily comic strip that is not a dramatic serial strip to develop a story over the course of more than six months is nearly unheard of. In the earlier days of *Nancy*, Ernie Bushmiller sometimes created story lines that ran for a few weeks, including stories about Nancy's acquisition of a pet pig in May 1943, but these stories never really served character development. The amount of time that Jaimes dedicates to Nancy and Esther's fight shows how central their relationship is to the strip.

While Esther is not speaking to Nancy, they each keep track of the other through lurking on their social media. What Kanai writes of female bloggers can be applied to the way *Nancy* displays Nancy and Esther's friendship: "We may observe the harmonious synthesis of defiance and pleasure, self-deprecation combined with claims of value, and a critical awareness of norms even as their impact is humorously managed and down-played."[42] On February 14, over the course of three panels, Nancy checks Esther's Facebook, Snapchat, and Instagram to see "if she's posted about our fight." In the fourth and final panel, Nancy says, "Better make sure she hasn't added anything to this message board she posted on in 2016." On March 16, 2019, Nancy and Esther speak briefly in school. Nancy tells Esther that she is working to become a famous artist. Esther replies, "Like I care." She then gives a detailed accounting of when Nancy has posted her art online before repeating, "I don't care at all."

Like *Nancy*, many other flexible comics focus, at least in part, on technology-mediated friendship. The "Slice of Life" comic section of the webcomic aggregator Tapas has more than sixteen thousand comics listed. The most popular comics, like Enzo's *Cheer Up, Emo Kid*, Cassandra Calin's *Cassandra Comics*, or Shen T.'s *Shen's Comics*, are syndicated on GoComics or available as print collections. Sarah Andersen's *Sarah's Scribbles* shares similarities with *Nancy* in the ways that its title character engages with the world. In a four-panel cartoon posted on Andersen's Facebook site on October 24, 2020, a young woman looking at her phone wonders in the first three panels what it means that "my friend doesn't try to converse but is always sending me memes." The final panel shows us Sarah, eyes wide and arms stretched out, staring at her own phone with the words "I LOVE YOU" in bold across the top of the panel. A *Sarah's Scribbles* from September 26, 2020, is called "Having a Friend Who Isn't Forever Online." This friend shows Sarah "a meme from four years ago" and says, "It's relatable." Sarah seems shocked that her friend does not realize that a four-year-old meme is hopelessly outdated.

When Jaimes focuses on Nancy's girlfriends in a pre-Halloween strip (October 30, 2020), Sluggo, alone in panel 1 of a three-panel strip, poses a question: "What would you say you're most afraid of?" The layout of this strip puts the focus on Nancy and her girlfriends. The first panel shows Sluggo close-up and is approximately one-third the size of the standard equal-sized three-panel comic. The subsequent two panels show Nancy, Agnes, Lucy, and Esther standing close together in equal-sized larger panels. The second panel shows all of the girls' thoughts as they contemplate Sluggo's question. Nancy thinks, "Clowns," but the others have more detailed thoughts that are all connected to friendship. Agnes thinks, "Being like everyone else." Her twin sister, Lucy, thinks, "Hurting a friend accidentally." Esther thinks, "Being hurt by my friends not being honest with me." Each of their thoughts has been rendered visible to readers, even as it remains invisible to Sluggo and to all the other girls. Readers can see the girls' relatable worries, even as the joke revealed in panel 3 is that all four girls say, "CLOWNS," in unison. Kanai writes that #relatable girls and young women must publicly face, and digitally perform, "the regulation of bodily femininity and injunctions to success, the feeling rules in relation to this regulation, as well as contrary feelings of dissatisfaction, inadequacy, frustration and ambivalence . . . to produce a relatable and representative self."[43] By simply making their thoughts visible, Jaimes shows that the girls care deeply about friendship, even if they remain ambivalent about sharing their thoughts. The four girls standing shoulder to shoulder in both panels and their collective response in the final panel put their affective bond on display. Kanai writes that "the replaying of mildly trying, everyday struggles works as an affective glue reassuring young women that they, too, are like other girlfriends who are getting by."[44] Kanai adds an important point regarding how young women and girls are able to get by, "although how one gets by as a young woman is markedly shaped by class and race as well as gender."[45] The picture of Nancy and her three girlfriends shows that Jaimes's representations of subjectivity include gender and race but not class. Their names, clothing, and hair mark their gender. Skin tones and hairstyles broadly define characters' race. Jaimes does not provide visual markings of social and economic class.

The markers of class that appeared in classic *Nancy*, such as Sluggo's accent, thread-worn clothing, and dilapidated house, do not appear in Jaimes's strip. All the kids' houses look generically similar, in a broadly defined middle-class way. Their homes all seem spacious, all the kids have private spaces and desks where they can do schoolwork, and they all have phones and computers. The class blindness of the strip speaks to a possible limit of relatability. The sameness of social and economic class in the strip seems to short-circuit any connection between class and relatability, as all the characters occupy the same class position. The jobs that the kids' parents and guardians have are only vaguely mentioned. Fritzi seems to have some sort of managerial position that involves an office and a laptop computer. Sluggo lives with his uncles (who never appear in the strip) and stays with Nancy when his uncles' undefined jobs keep them "on the road." Agnes and Lucy's mother appears in a few strips, but her job is never mentioned. Esther lives with her older sister, but no mention of her parents is ever made. In some ways, the vagueness of the adult world is a continuation of *Nancy*'s legacy. From Bushmiller to Jaimes, *Nancy* has never discussed why Nancy lives with her aunt and not her parents. The working life of parents and guardians obviously plays a huge role in the determination of economic class. In not focusing on this aspect of life, Jaimes's *Nancy* remains silent on questions of how class shapes identity. *Nancy*'s world is one of an idealized and shared middle-class.

Black Representation in Comics

In a legacy comic like *Nancy*, histories of representation haunt the present. Abate shows in *Funny Girls* that early and mid-twentieth-century comics were overwhelmingly white. She writes, "All the Funny Girls who permeated this era are white. As a result, female protagonists like Little Lulu, Little Audrey, and L'il Tomboy worked to challenge the gender line, but not the racial one."[46] Abate argues that considering the absence of main characters of color and the racial stereotypes that these strips often employed as "products of their time" would be a mistake: "Instead, they reveal the highly racialized way that childhood, girlhood, and especially innocence were constructed, disseminated, and reinforced in the United States during these eras."[47] In the same way, then, racial representations in contemporary comics likewise construct, disseminate, and reinforce specific ways of being in the world.

More broadly, racial representation and racism have been part of American comics since their inception. Rebecca Wanzo, in *The Content of Our Caricature*, writes that American comics have developed an "expansive visual grammar about identity" that "uses racialized caricature as a mechanism for constructing both ideal and undesirable types of citizens."[48] From the nineteenth century through the middle of the twentieth century, racist caricatures were rife in American comics. In his foreword to Fredrik Strömberg's *Black Images in the Comics: A Visual History*, Charles Johnson writes, "As a black American reader my visceral reaction to this barrage of racist drawings from the 1840s through the 1940s was revulsion and a profound sadness."[49] In their "Analysis of Black Images in Comic Strips, 1915–1995," Sylvia E. White and Tania Fuentez write that it was not until the late 1960s and early 1970s "that strips using race relations as a major theme for humor began to appear, including strips like *Wee Pals*, by Morrie Turner, and *Quincy*, by Ted Shearer, [which] both featured an integrated group of children."[50] The 1960s and '70s marked the emergence of many Black comic superheroes, including Marvel's Falcon, Black Panther, and Luke Cage and DC's Green Lantern, John Stewart. Adilifu Nama, in his book *Super Black: American Pop Culture and Black Superheroes*, argues that "broad and sweeping cultural trends of American politics and pop culture during the 1960s and 1970s [were a] significant catalyst for the appearance of black superheroes."[51]

Charles Schulz did not introduce Franklin, the first Black character in *Peanuts*, until 1968. Charlie Brown meets Franklin on a beach on July 31; the next day, Charlie Brown invites Franklin to his house. Many people have noted that Franklin remained a relatively bland character over the years.[52] In a 1977 interview with Stan Isaacs, Schulz rhetorically asks, "What do I know about what it is like to be black?"[53] Rebecca Wanzo notes that "for Schulz, gender is apparently less of an obstacle to identification than is race," as he has no trouble imaging the lives of white girls, even as he states that he cannot imagine the life of a Black boy.[54] Yet Schulz's inclusion of a Black character helps show that representation does indeed matter in comic strips. Barbara Brandon-Craft, the first Black woman to have a "nationally syndicated comic strip in the mainstream press," told David Kamp that as a ten-year-old in 1968, "I remember feeling affirmed by seeing Franklin in 'Peanuts.' There's a little black kid! Thank goodness! We *do* matter."[55] Robb Armstrong, the creator of *Jump Start*, "one of the most widely syndicated black comic strips ever [and still running today]," was a child in 1968 and says of encountering Franklin in *Peanuts*, "He inspired some kid 3,000 miles away. . . . It's incredible what happens when you inspire a kid, and that's what Schulz did."[56] Armstrong later sent Schulz a comic strip, and they became friends. In the 1990s Schulz realized that Franklin did not have a last name. He asked Armstrong if he could give Franklin his last name, and Armstrong said he was "in awe 'of the tremendous honor."[57] According to Armstrong, Schulz was very supportive of *Jump Start*, in part because "on some level, he knew he had inspired me and that I would be speaking about this black family in ways he never could."[58]

Amid these changing social mores about representations of Black characters in comics, Bushmiller was more ambivalent about including a Black character in Nancy. In *How to Read "Nancy,"* Karasik and Newgarden write that in the early 1970s "Bushmiller found himself under increasing editorial pressure from his syndicate to introduce a black youngster into his insular cast."[59] It seems, though, that Bushmiller must have been at least unconsciously aware of racial representation in *Nancy* well before the 1970s. In her chapter on Bushmiller's *Nancy*, Abate makes the provocative and convincing claim that Bushmiller's *Nancy* "is an amalgamation of vaudevillian elements."[60] Abate focuses on how both vaudeville and Bushmiller's strip were seen as "lowbrow" forms of entertainment that employ gag humor, linguistic misunderstandings, and dialect, but I am more interested in her claim that "the elements of vaudeville in *Nancy* add a new facet to discussions of class, ethnicity, and race in the comic."[61] Abate draws a strong connection between Bushmiller's *Nancy* and "blackface minstrelsy," especially regarding Nancy's hair: "Her signature frizzy coif . . . strongly resembles both the woolly wigs worn by minstrel performers and the highly minstrelized way that young black children were rendered in advertisements."[62] In *Birth of an Industry: Blackface Minstrelsy and the Rise of American Animation*, Nicholas Sammond calls this "vestigial minstrelsy." He writes that cartoon characters in the 1930s, such as Mickey Mouse, carried "the tokens of blackface minstrelsy in their bodies and behaviors yet [were] no longer immediately signifying as such," since live minstrelsy was falling out of favor.[63] While audience awareness of the conventions of minstrelsy diminished, cartoons still "maintain[ed] minstrelsy as a vestigial element stripped of its explicit connotations."[64] For example, Abate notes that the recurring character Marigold, one of Nancy's nemeses, is "dressed in a manner that mirrors one of the most famous minstrel performers: Jim Crow," and she then draws a strong parallel between a well-known lithograph of "Jim Crow" and the way that Marigold dances in Bushmiller's November 16, 1941, strip.[65] Abate also points to the times when Nancy falls in mud or puts on Aunt Fritzi's "beauty mud" so that she appears to be wearing blackface. Similarly, Bushmiller's April 3, 1946, strip shows Sluggo's head covered in paint in a way that could be taken as blackface; the final panel shows an outline of Sluggo's completely blacked-out face, except for his white, wide grin. In 1966, Abate notes, Bushmiller uses the same joke, with Nancy appearing in blackface. The social context surrounding representations of race in 1966 varies quite a bit from that of 1946. The reuse of this particular joke does not consider changing views about racial representations.

The 1946 strip can be seen in an appendix in Karasik and Newgarden's *How to Read "Nancy"* that compiles various strips that illustrate some of Bushmiller's formal techniques. This strip is part of the category "Spotting Blacks," with the subheading "Solid Blacks Emphasize." The strip in question, then, serves as an illustration of how Bushmiller uses black ink in the strip to create emphasis. In that context, this strip is a perfect example of his use of black ink, as the spilled paint forms a solid block of black ink over Sluggo. Viewed purely from a formalist perspective, this strip suggests nothing more than a joke about spilled paint. But as Aaron Meskin points out in his essay "Defining Comics?," formalism always runs the risk of "its failure to take into account the historical contexts in which works of art are produced."[66] Even as part of a formalist analysis of Bushmiller's style, the title "Spotting Blacks" seems unfortunate in the way that it plays off the racialized valences of Bushmiller's *Nancy*. In their introduction to *The Blacker the Ink*, Frances Gateward and John Jennings write about the "openness and mutability of ink" as an element of comics' production.[67] They argue that "the ink used in comics is not only physically and formally perceived to be the neutral of black; it also is the reification of 'Blackness' in the modern sense."[68] They note that the act of applying black ink to a white bristol board marks the ways that Blackness and whiteness get represented on the page: "When a drop of ink hits a white piece of paper, something happens. . . . It defines the whiteness of the page, and in turn, the whiteness of the page begins to define it."[69] For Gateward and Jennings, capitalism obscures the process of creation in favor of the final product that can be "printed, mass marketed, and consumed."[70] This creative process is never just formalist. It is always a part of the social and cultural ideologies surrounding it.

Bushmiller saw himself as a formalist, and his reluctance to include a Black character in *Nancy* can be read as a formalist blind spot and as a refutation of his work's social context (remember his statement, "I have never gotten an idea from real life"). In a 1973 article, James Carrier notes that comics like Charles Schulz's *Peanuts* and Mort Walker's *Beetle Bailey* had recently introduced Black characters, Franklin and Lt. Fuzz, respectively. Other critics, such as Fredrik Strömberg, have noted that many newspaper comics introduced Black characters in the 1960s and 1970s. Carrier notes that "Ernie Bushmiller, the 64-year-old creator of 'Nancy,' says integration has been troubling him." Bushmiller says, "My instincts tell me to do it. I'm waiting. I want the strip to be pleasant. I think it would be forced in *Nancy*. I read the comics for enjoyment. *Pogo* is a social comment. Mine isn't. Mine is Lawrence Welk."[71] Bushmiller died in 1982 without having introduced a Black character in *Nancy*. His words show that introducing a Black character into *Nancy* would have been political. The opposition he draws between "pleasant" comics read for "enjoyment" and the "social comment" of a strip like *Pogo* implies that including a Black character would have been a kind of social comment. Not including one makes its own social comment.

A brief consideration of reactions to Black superhero comics can make this clear.

In her essay "American Truths: Blackness and the American Superhero," Consuela Francis focuses on readers' perceptions of Black superheroes, particularly in the 2002 Captain America series, *Truth: Red, White, and Black*. This series tells the story of a group of Black soldiers who were secretly injected with the same supersoldier serum that Steve Rogers voluntarily takes. The series was "based largely on the Tuskegee syphilis experiments, in which . . . the U.S. Public Health Service conducted an experiment on 399 black men in the late stages of syphilis, without their knowledge."[72] Rebecca Wanzo writes that the Black Captain America of *Truth* is "an inherently ambiguous figure" who struggles to be patriotic even as he is "betrayed by the US government."[73] Francis writes that a Marvel editor said some of the strongest reactions to the series came from "outright racists who just don't like the idea of a black man in the Cap uniform."[74] Considering *Truth* and other comics that center on Black superheroes, Francis writes that many fans were worried that that Black superheroes were often "poorly done and/or over politicized."[75] She argues that a more important point underlies these negative reactions to Black superheroes: "Readers' assumption that black equals political and that political equals bad or, at least, unentertaining, art."[76] These readers' reactions, as characterized by Francis, mirror Bushmiller's claims that comics should be simply pleasant and entertaining.

Colorblind Representation

Jaimes's *Nancy* has a diverse group of characters, even as Jaimes's minimalistic style does not focus on the kinds of realistic details that might visually define a specific character's race or ethnicity. Nonetheless, her attention to skin tones and hair type and style shows that the world of her comic is not monochromatic. Nancy,

Sluggo, and Fritzi have been considered "white" throughout the run of the strip, and the pinkish-white skin tone Jaimes gives them does nothing to change that perception. Sluggo's shaved head and Fritzi's curly hair signify little about racial representation. Nancy's unnamed math teacher, introduced on May 7, 2018, is portrayed with light-brown skin and black hair pulled into a ponytail. Nancy's friend Esther has black hair, like Nancy's, but Esther's hair is straight and long with a small part on one side. Esther has browner skin than Nancy. Nancy's identical twin friends, Agnes and Lucy, appear to be represented as Black. Their skin tone is darker than Esther's. Agnes and Lucy both wear their hair natural. Lucy often sports afro puffs, and Agnes sometimes wears a loose ponytail or has her hair pushed behind her ears. Jaimes does not draw her characters with a lot of realistic detail, but it seems clear that within the limited cartoon variance of *Nancy*, characters' skin tones and hairstyles represent racial differences. As I note earlier in this chapter, Jaimes does not visually represent class on the page. Likewise, she does not show race as an influence on characters' interactions and experiences. This kind of representation has been called colorblind or post-racial.

In her 2019 book, *Colorblind Racism*, Meghan Burke writes that "colorblind racism asserts that there are no real problems with racism in our society . . . ignoring our often drastically different starting points towards achieving success, or the prevalence of ongoing forms of racism and bias that persist in everyday life."[77] Colorblind racism exists in multiple contexts, such as institutions, including health care, school, and criminal justice; legal policies, including housing, education, and immigration; and cultural contexts, including family life and popular culture. Burke writes that colorblind racism occurs "when we ignore or distrust the regular and patterned experiences of those who are marginalized by these systems, preferring inaccurate explanations that perhaps make us more comfortable or that come to be seen as common sense."[78] Jaimes's *Nancy* places all its characters in very similar educational and family contexts, as I discuss above. The strip never mentions that a character's race has an effect on their life in any direct way. Even as Jaimes's strip uses a colorblind ideology, though, it does some interesting work in the context of daily comic strips.

Burke writes that "the expression of colorblindness is not always done uncritically, and is often shaped by additional contexts and strategies that reflect meaningful personal choices, and even resistance to the racial status quo."[79] The racial status quo of daily syndicated comic strips rarely includes the representation of friend groups of different races. White and Fuentez write that, as recently as 1995, while comic strips no longer trafficked in "negative stereotypes, [and] black characters appear[ed] in a broader range of jobs and social settings than ever before . . . blacks are seriously underrepresented in daily newspaper comic strips," with most strips that they surveyed containing no Black characters.[80] In her essay "Contemporary Representations of Black Females in Newspaper Comic Strips," Tia T. M. Cyree analyzes the appearance of Black female characters in "13 newspaper comics . . . during January and February 2011."[81] She notes that "in total, eight Black female children and one teenager occupied either minor or major roles."[82] *Nancy*'s world in 2019 is more diverse than that of most well-known daily comic strips. Jaimes's presentation of race is purely pictorial, visualized through skin tone and hairstyle. All of Jaimes's characters speak the same way, and she does not use racial stereotypes to establish characters' backgrounds. Jaimes's portrayal of race may be superficial, but it is visible. In a comic strip world where "black comic strip characters seem caught in perpetual non-recognition," Agnes, Lucy, and Esther do matter, as readers see characters of color represented on the page.[83] Jaimes's

Nancy contributes to a more inclusive space of comic strips and takes a small step toward changing daily comics' legacy of unreflective whiteness. In Jaimes's *Nancy*, racial representation is a matter of being seen in both extra- and intradiegetic ways.

Within the world of the strip, Jaimes also emphasizes the everyday ways that representations of difference matter. When they are together, Nancy, Agnes, and Lucy spend a lot of time drawing. They all create and draw characters with superpowers, and Jaimes represents their artwork in the strip. Lucy creates "Infinitia," and Agnes creates "Serenity." Serenity has wings, a crown, and blue hair, while Infinitia has wings and flowing, purple hair. Both characters have the same skin color as their creators. Nancy creates "Nanciana," an older, cooler version of herself, with red bow, black spiky hair, and white skin. These characters show that children often see themselves in their creations. But in the December 19, 2018, strip, Lucy and Nancy exchange Christmas presents. Nancy has drawn a picture of Lucy's Infinitia, and Lucy has drawn a picture of Nanciana. Each draws the other's character with the "correct" skin color. Nancy's Infinitia has brown skin, and Lucy's Nanciana has white skin. These representations show that while race plays a small role in *Nancy*, the characters within the strip do see racial difference. Skin tone and hairstyle exist intradiegetically, as shown in the girls' drawings of each other. Race exists, but it does not seem to have meaning for them. As Nancy looks at Lucy's gift, she thinks, "It's sweet that she tried, but everybody knows Nanciana has 46 hair spikes, not 49." The minute difference of three hair spikes makes the punch line about Nancy's narcissism, but it does not erase the inclusivity of the strip. To use Bushmiller's language once more, Jaimes has no gag about a Black kid. But the absence of a gag no longer means the absence of a Black kid in *Nancy*. The kids of color in Jaimes's *Nancy* serve the humor of the strip as part of Nancy's cohort, not as racialized types.

While representation in a simply drawn comic like *Nancy* works differently than it does in superhero comics, the character of Lunella Lafayette, the preteen heroine of *Moon Girl and Devil Dinosaur*, can serve as an example of why representations of Blackness in superhero comics are also important in comics like *Nancy* and how colorblindness can be understood in different ways. Eric Berlatsky and Sika Dagbovie-Mullins describe Lunella, who "sports natural hair and wears round glasses" so that she "presents as a preteen black hipster."[84] Putting aside her superpowers and dinosaur friend, she seems like a character who would be at home in Jaimes's *Nancy*—she is in the same age group and enjoys inventing things. She would fit right into the robotics club.[85] Likewise, the way her race is represented in *Moon Girl* bears similarities to racial representation in *Nancy*. Berlatsky and Dagbovie-Mullins note that "Lunella's hair acts as an important signifier of 'authentic' blackness."[86] And like Esther, Agnes, and Lucy, Lunella's "race plays no significant role in the stories told in the first two volumes of *Moon Girl*. . . . She could easily be any race or ethnicity."[87] Berlatsky and Dagbovie-Mullins argue that Lunella "is a remarkably post-racial figure, as her adventures rarely if ever explicitly explore the vexed politics of race."[88] At the same time, they argue that certain racist ideologies such as Black male criminality and "white male ownership of black women . . . are inscribed within" *Moon Girl*, thus complicating the racial politics of the comic.[89] In her "Representation Matters: Post-Racial Tensions in *Moon Girl and Devil Dinosaur*," Mary J. Henderson criticizes the post-racial aspects of *Moon Girl* that deemphasize the role that race plays in Lunella's life. Henderson writes that *Moon Girl* "offers a conservative representation of Black girlhood that can be both empowering for readers and dismissive of the social injustices that may impact such a character. . . . The comic can showcase a gifted African American girl, and yet ignore the systematic racism and issues facing an inner city Black child."[90] At the same time, Henderson says that *Moon Girl* "is a progressive comic on many levels."[91] The comic avoids blatant stereotypes and is "culturally nuanced" in comparison to earlier portrayals of Black woman and girl superheroes. *Moon Girl* uses a "spectrum of shades" to illustrate skin tones that mirror real-world appearances. Henderson shows that a comic can both miss opportunities to show how systematic racism can affect nonwhite characters and represent racial difference as it appears in the real world. Even as comics might ignore important social and cultural aspects of race, they can create means of relatability through representation.

In her essay about the superhero comic *The Life and Times of America Chavez*, Laura M. Jiménez explains the value of Latina representations in comics. Identifying herself as a "Latina lesbian" reader, Jiménez writes, "I recognized myself in America in ways I had never experienced in comics."[92] Written by Gabby Rivera, a "queer Latinx" author, and drawn by "well-known Latino artists," America Chavez "succeeded by giving authentic voice to queer women of color."[93] Chavez's authenticity comes from the same place as the #OwnVoices movement's call for works created by authors (and artists) who share the same diverse identity as their characters.[94] The identity-based correlation between creators, characters, and readers helps Jiménez to state, "I saw myself" when reading this comic.[95] Rivera's America Chavez is relatable. Readers can identify with the character and see a version of themselves reflected back. This kind of relatability leads to a rich reading experience. Wanda Brooks argues that "culturally influenced textual features have the potential to become important pedagogical tools for literary instruction."[96] Brooks studies how an ethnically diverse group of middle school students relates to "culturally conscious" African American children's books.[97] In looking at student responses that focused on "previously identified recurring themes, linguistic patterns, and ethnic group practices," Brooks explores how students responded to specific "African-American textual features" of the books.[98] These responses showed that both individual experiences and ethnic identity contributed to students' interpretations. Brooks describes how the "African-American students . . . drew on their cultural knowledge and experiences to construct interpretations," while stating that "even for children of a similar ethnicity who read representations of themselves, cultural complexity must be acknowledged from the beginning."[99] This cultural complexity accounts for differing individual reading experiences, even as many students identified with characters whom they saw as representations of their identities. Reading a text as #relatable can be seen as an entry point to understanding and interpreting that text. At the same time, relatability does not erase individual differences within larger groups.

Nancy and her friends' relatability is complicated by Jaimes's pseudonymity. *Nancy* cannot be considered a #OwnVoices text, simply because readers do not know Jaimes's ethnic and racial identity. As I note in my introduction, Jaimes's gender identity as the first woman creator of *Nancy* is emphasized over any other aspect of identity. While Nancy, Esther, Agnes, and Lucy represent diverse racial identities, they do not offer a strong identity-based connection that would produce the sense of authenticity that Jiménez locates between the shared identity of creator, character, and reader. Nevertheless, in the often overwhelming whiteness of daily cartoon characters, Jaimes's character diversity matters, especially when one considers *Nancy*'s legacy of racial caricature grounded in vestigial minstrelsy.

Nancy's legacy brings with it a long material history of gender and racial representations. Jaimes confronts this legacy by producing new representations that reflect contemporary sensibilities. Some nostalgic readers might view these changes negatively, while newer readers might not even be aware of *Nancy*'s legacy. Especially in her "new" Fritzi, Jaimes anticipates and defuses critical comments, which lays the groundwork for her rethinking the gender dynamics of the strip. Jaimes's *Nancy* also shows that a pure formalism that refuses to address current realities of representation simply does not work in contemporary flexible comics. In the next chapter, I will explore how Jaimes's *Nancy* uses various kinds of objects, from cookie jars to phone screens, to create humor for both nostalgic and new readers. Like her reconfiguration of gender and racial representation, Jaimes uses technological objects to reconfigure the ways that humor works in the strip. Just as she pays close attention to the histories of gender and race encoded in *Nancy*'s legacy, Jaimes refers to the historically humorous use of objects like ladders as her strip works to make material history #relatable, and funny, to contemporary readers.

3
"But I Broke the Fourth Wall!"

Nancy's Object Humor (January 20, 2019)

Cookie Jars and Metacomics

Jaimes's January 20, 2019, *Nancy* uses multiple objects—a cookie jar, a ladder, a newspaper, the gutter between panels—and only a few words to create a humorous metacomic. This is a Sunday strip, so Jaimes has more visual space than in a daily comic to develop the joke. Seven of the eight panels of this strip do not have speech balloons. The panels are arranged in a two-by-four grid (four rows of two panels). The conceit of the joke is a simple and familiar one to newspaper comic strip readers: a character desires a forbidden cookie jar that has been placed out of reach. Cookie jars became popular in the United States in the 1930s, and comic strips have been using them to signify desire for an unattainable object for nearly as long.[1] Ernie Bushmiller's *Nancy* used the cookie jar trope numerous times; in the 1950s and 1960s Mort Walker's *Hi and Lois*, Charles Schulz's *Peanuts*, and Hank Ketchum's *Dennis the Menace* employed it often. The trope has been a staple of Jim Davis's *Garfield* since the 1970s and was common in Bill Watterson's *Calvin and Hobbes* in the 1980s and 1990s. Creators like Jaimes continue to use it in the twenty-first century. Even as the symbolic function of the cookie jar remains clear to comic readers, the materiality of cookie jars has certainly changed since the 1940s. A cookie jar in a kitchen seems like a relic of

1950s Americana, as it signifies homemade cookies baked by a stay-at-home mother with time on her hands to bake. Cookie jars have little utility in a time of readily available packaged cookies, except as a marker of nostalgia. (Likewise, many mid-twentieth-century comic strips used homemade cakes and pies as similar symbols of desire, and many nostalgic comic strips still do.) In this particular *Nancy* strip, Nancy uses a ladder to get to a cookie jar that sits atop the refrigerator. The strip can be read as a metacomic, because Nancy also uses the gutters between panels and the layout of the panels on the page to reach the cookie jar. Nancy seems to leave the two-dimensional space of the strip as a means to get a cookie.

An incongruous ladder appears out of nowhere in panel 2 of the strip. The absurdity of the ladder's appearance fits neatly into the conventions of comic strips. As Pascal Lefèvre notes, "In a humorous drawn comic the reader will accept more voluntary inconsistencies in the representation of the diegetic space."[2] We do not need to know exactly how the ladder got to this space; we take its appearance for granted. Ladders in comics offer many possibilities for humor (falling off the ladder, climbing to an inaccessible space and surprising someone, etc.), which seems to be the point in this strip. A ladder appears; something funny will ensue.

Nancy climbs the ladder in panel 3 and reaches across the gutter to grab the cookie jar in panel 4 and throw it to herself. Both Nancy and the cookie jar cross over the edge of panel 4, with great consequence for readers. Our assumption of synchronous time moving left to right and top to bottom, from panel to panel, is disrupted as the Nancy in panel 3 is able to throw the cookie jar to the Nancy in panel 4, as if they exist simultaneously. Likewise, a reader's sense of the strip as a three-dimensional illusion drawn in two-dimensional space goes flying with the cookie jar. The illusion of depth that we unconsciously see—Nancy in the kitchen and Fritzi in a room adjacent to the kitchen—gives way to another, denser illusion. Nancy in panel 3 seems to have anchored herself with her left leg along the right edge of panel 3, but part of her foot goes into the three-dimensional space outside the panel. Even as the panel lines and gutters have become a physical part of Nancy's world (i.e., they exist within her two-dimensional frame of reference, or she wouldn't be able to move across and through them), the gutter still serves its traditional purpose of denoting the passage of time between panels. The gutter serves as both diegetic and extradiegetic space. It separates panels, but it is also a part of panels 3 and 4. In her desire to reach the cookie jar, Nancy has overcome logic and the rules of how space and time work in the comic strip.

Nancy's triumph as she eats a cookie would seem to be the end of the joke, but Aunt Fritzi has seen what Nancy has done. Nancy, shocked that she has been caught, says, "But I broke the fourth wall! How could you see me?" This question seems to be the punch line. Nancy has gone meta, noting that she is in a comic strip by saying she broke through the invisible space between strip and reader. But Fritzi has an answer for Nancy's question. She holds up the newspaper and shows Nancy that she has been reading *Nancy* in the Sunday comic section, which allowed her to see what Nancy was up to in panels 1–7. Panel 8 shows us the back of Nancy's head as she looks at the newspaper. Her head obscures part of the comic page, but we can see that the comic Aunt Fritzi has just read is a representation of the same comic that we have just read. At least on this day, *Nancy* exists within the world of *Nancy*.

And there is still one more incongruity. This comic strip is laid out online in four rows of two panels each. The *Nancy* that appears in Aunt Fritzi's newspaper in panel 8 is made up of nine panels, with three rows of three panels. There is an extra panel in the newspaper comic. Looking closely, panels 1 and 2 of the online comic correspond to the first two panels of the newspaper comic within the strip. Panel 3 of Aunt Fritzi's newspaper comic has no corresponding panel in the actual comic strip. The rest of the panels match up, so that panels 4–9 of the newspaper strip within the strip match up to panels 3–8 of the actual strip. Panel 3 of the newspaper comic within the strip is partially obscured by Nancy's head in panel 8 of the actual comic, so readers can only see the left side of the panel, where the refrigerator is. We cannot see the ladder or Nancy. Regardless, this panel exists only in the newspaper strip within *Nancy*. In eight (or nine?) panels, Jaimes has constructed a multilevel metacomic that humorously and continually undermines readers' assumptions about the basic conventions of comic strips. Of course, metahumor itself is a comic strip convention of long standing. While metacomics are as old as comics themselves, contemporary uses of metahumor like Jaimes's work differently than in twentieth-century comics.

Comic scholar Thomas Inge writes that metahumor in comics has a long history, dating back to Richard Outcault's *Yellow Kid* in 1895. Inge shows that Outcault's humor "becomes complex" because we laugh at the titular character commenting on the actions of the children who appear in the strip. Inge notes that Outcault occasionally increased the strip's complexity by having the Yellow Kid hold up a note from the "artist" so that "the fictional mediator becomes a personal messenger as a part of the playful scheme."[3] Inge argues that metahumor was used occasionally in comics through the early and mid-twentieth century (even citing an Ernie Bushmiller *Nancy* strip as one example) but increases in "variety and frequency" in the latter part of the twentieth century.[4] One type of comic metahumor Inge analyzes is self-reflexive metacomics: "those which reflect on and use as a source of humor the technical conventions of the comic strip—the materials of production, such as pencils, pens, ink, and paper; the borders or panels and the placement of dialogue in balloon."[5] Inge's article was published in 1991, before online comics and digital drawing tools altered these "technical conventions," but his definition still works for contemporary, flexible metacomics. He concludes that metacomics "can be used to make serious statements about the larger scheme of things"[6] and that "the real world, then, like the comic strip, is but a reflection of existence and neither is more substantial nor permanent than the other."[7] In other words, metahumor can serve to level the field of representation. The "real world" and the comic strip exist in the same material space and neither precedes the other or offers a more fundamental view of things. They are objects forging connections with each other. The complexity of metacomics leaves them open to reflection, rereading, and recontextualizing. The newspaper comic section that Aunt Fritzi points to invites readers into the space of the comic, as both Fritzi and the reader are reading *Nancy*. At the same time, the extra panel in Fritzi's newspaper comic and the fact that most readers are probably reading *Nancy* on a screen push readers out of the space of the strip.

New and Old Objects

Eszter Szép argues that metacomics resist, or at least extend, Scott McCloud's famous definition of closure in comics: "the operation by which the reader connects adjacent panels, and thus creates the story."[8] Szép claims that closure almost always happens automatically as "it is a learned and rehearsed activity."[9] Metacomics, for Szép, are one place where closure is not automatic. In these instances, "the reader [is] forced to reflect on his or her role, on the structure of the specific work that is read, or on the nature of comics in general."[10] Jaimes's *Nancy* certainly leads readers to reflect on the role they play in telling a story or making meaning from comics. But the work of closure, or of leaving closure open to possibility, goes beyond the relationship between creator and reader in flexible comics like *Nancy*. Szép writes that "the very form and the unit of the page is open to reveal and reconsider its own structure."[11] If flexible comics expand the notion of the page to include the screen, then this openness multiplies. Szép suggests that metacomics can never exhaust their possibilities, writing, "The number of such self-reflexive gestures are infinite."[12] So when comics like *Nancy* embrace the metatextual properties of both print comics (ink, paper, pages) and digital comics (pixels, screens, iconography), they increase the possibilities of metacomics.

It is precisely in this possibility of "infinite" gestures that I want to locate the potential for contemporary flexible comics to say something new. Comics like Jaimes's *Nancy* resist closure through the ways that characters interact with different types of objects. The objects of the strip I discuss at the top of this chapter—cookie jars, ladders, newspapers themselves—have been staples of newspaper comics throughout the twentieth century. I call these old objects, to contrast them with the new technological objects that contemporary comic strips use to create metahumor. Flexible comic creators like Jaimes use both traditional objects that would seem commonplace in mid-twentieth-century comics and technological objects that firmly place the strip in its twenty-first-century context. Old objects include cookie jars, rocks, eyeglasses, clothes, food, animals, pets, hats, windows, fences, hoses, plants, trees, swings, slides, and drawings done on paper. New objects include mobile phones, laptop computers, drawings done on screens, and things that appear on computer screens, such as web forms, Wikipedia pages, Snapchat filters, Instagram pages, icons, and video-chat backgrounds. While these new objects often appear in traditional legacy strips like *Blondie* or *Beetle Bailey*, they usually do not serve as a central focus of humor or characterization in such strips. New technologies do not shape the subjectivities of characters in such legacy strips, as many of these characters think and act in the same ways that they have for decades. Contemporary webcomics and flexible comics like *Nancy*, *Sarah's Scribbles*, and *Strange Planet*, however, use new objects as both the focus of their humor and as a way to show characters' emotions and ways of interacting with the world. For instance, on November 28, 2020, *Sarah's Scribbles* uses the "love" icon of a heart as a material object in the strip. Sarah says that her friends can post "a picture of <u>anything</u>" and she "will be ready." As her friend posts a picture of a sandwich, the final panel of the strip shows Sarah holding a heart icon above her head, as if the icon is a physical object that she can throw at a social media post. Comics like *Nancy* that are both flexible and legacy use old and new objects in novel configurations to produce humorous results.

The ways that comic creators use technology to reflect on their roles as creators can further illustrate the differences between old and new metahumor. Szép notes the long tradition of comic creators representing themselves at their drawing desk, especially in autobiographical comics such as Lynda Barry's work. Szép writes that "scenes showing the artists themselves sitting at their desks, creating the very comics the reader is holding, are abundant."[13] Such scenes, Szép writes, can serve one of two purposes: "Such moments can be interpreted either as access to an original subjectivity via the act of drawing or as visualizations and mediations of the birth of the line."[14] These self-representations serve as a mark of authenticity and embodiment, whether it is of the author's self or body or the lines that are drawn on the page by that self or body. At the beginning of chapter 1, I discuss the "Artist's Note" that Jaimes sometimes uses in *Nancy*. These notes, and especially a "Cartoonist Note" that Jaimes uses at the end of a strip, might seem to serve as a similar establishment of the creator's presence in the work. At the same time, this is not to overlook the important distinction that Szép's focus is nonfiction comics, where authenticity and presence work differently than they do in fictional strips. Olivia Jaimes writing under a pseudonym further shows that her notes are a performative part of creating her persona.

Before the "Cartoonist Note" appears in the final panel of the four-panel April 16, 2018, strip, Sluggo tells Nancy, "You look a little . . . off." Both Sluggo and Nancy are poorly drawn in the first three panels. Their proportions are wrong; they seem to not have necks; they are not looking at each other while they are talking; they do not move from panel to panel. In panel 2 Nancy says, "I think the cartoonist is having an off day." Her words are struck through with a line in panel 2, though, as if she says the words but then the cartoonist thinks better of it but cannot revise and start over. Nancy's words are under erasure, which makes it difficult to know how to read them. Should readers read them and then forget them, as if they have not been said? Instead of the cartoonist having a bad drawing day, we learn from Nancy in panel 3, "Actually this is just a Snapchat filter."[15] A reader's knowledge of what a "Snapchat filter" is once again brings up issues of relatability. Users of Snapchat would easily relate to this claim, while less technologically literate readers might not get the joke. The "Cartoonist Note" of panel 4 explains that "any questionable art from now on is because Nancy and Sluggo are using a Snapchat filter." In striking through Nancy's words and adding a note at the end of the strip, Jaimes asserts her presence as an artist and a writer. Jaimes's self-reference does not serve to guarantee her authenticity in either body or drawn line, however. Instead, Jaimes draws readers' attention to technological mediation in her creation. The cartoonist disavows responsibility for any "questionable art" that may later appear in the strip. Here, Jaimes connects to the jokes centered on her persona's self-assurance of her artistic ability, as I discussed in chapter 1. Once again, she asserts confidence in the face of possible failure; "confidence culture" lets her ascribe any drawing problems not to herself but to a computer-generated filter. At the same time, Jaimes shows that her humor is flexible, as the joke is rooted in an older comic trope related to pen-and-ink drawing and representations of authorial voice.

It is important to note that a Snapchat filter and a writer's desk are both material objects. In *Comics and the Senses*, Ian Hague writes that while "it is tempting to understand digital formats as transparent mediums of transmission, windows onto a media landscape . . . digital manifestations of images do have a physicality to them."[16] This physicality might not be as readily apparent; one can hold a pencil in one's hand, whereas the physical aspects of a Snapchat filter (the computer code that manipulates an image on a screen) are not ready to hand in the same way. Yet both have a real, material presence. Aaron Kashtan makes this point in a different way in *Between Pen and Pixel*. Discussing the photographs of Lynda Barry's collages of everyday objects from her book *What It Is*, Kashtan reminds readers that while Barry's actual collage did contain pieces of pajamas, the book contains "*photographs* of pieces of pajamas."[17] These digitally reproduced photographs, not the pieces of pajamas, have a material reality for readers who "must touch the pages in order to read the book, and [they are] therefore necessarily aware that the pages feel smooth and flat."[18] In other words, the pages of the book do not just offer a representation of the photographed collage; they have their own "smooth and flat" presence. Comic theory has tended to pay more attention to old objects like book pages, but this seems to be changing as critics focus on the contemporary material conditions of comic creation. In *Comics and Stuff* Henry Jenkins purposefully keeps his definition of "stuff" quite broad: "the accumulated things that constitute our familiar surroundings."[19] "Stuff," for Jenkins, is a way of thinking about material culture, and he mostly focuses on the collections and accumulations of stuff that happen over lifetimes. Most of the stuff he focuses on fits into the category of old objects—vinyl records, antique toys, early and mid-twentieth-century comic books—as these things become part of a collection and obtain value. Jenkins makes the key point that the visual aspect of comics means precisely that every visible object in a comic was put there purposefully. He writes, "This stuff is not drawn by accident," even if it might seem like unimportant background information that we might not even notice on a first read.[20] While Jenkins, in his choice of graphic novels, focuses mostly on old "stuff," there is no reason that his argument cannot work for new objects as well.

In fact, Zara Dinnen, in "Things That Matter: Representing Everyday Technological Things in Comics," argues that comics can be especially apt in their representations of contemporary technical objects like computers and mobile phones. She writes that "graphic narratives offer a particular set of representational tools for depicting the digital in all its complex thingliness."[21] Following Bill Brown and Bruno Latour, Dinnen draws a distinction between "things" and "objects." In this formulation, "things" will "exceed the status of objects, but are not fully procedural, or systematic; they retain mass and form but resist categorization and naming."[22] Dinnen demonstrates that graphic narratives can show the ways that computers are more than just inert objects: "Thinking of computers as things enables an artistic and critical approach that gathers together disparate concerns: the materiality of digital culture, the corporate branding and protocols of that culture, personal interaction with devices and networks."[23]

Things form connections; they link to other things; they are networked. Because of their ability to form these linkages, things resist wholeness—you cannot grasp every aspect of a computer just by looking at it. Something about it is always withdrawn. Dinnen writes that a desktop computer represented in Danica Novgorodoff's 2009 graphic novel *Refresh Refresh* is "always performing in excess or anticipation of its networked entity."[24] I argue, following object-oriented ontologists like Graham Harman and Timothy Morton, that all objects, not just technical ones, are "withdrawn" in this way. All objects exceed or anticipate their immediate possibilities. A cookie jar, for instance, does not reveal all its possible linkages to us when we see one. We cannot always know what is inside it, who may form a connection to it, or where that connection might lead. We do not know in advance how far a character like Nancy will go to reach a cookie jar on a high shelf. This ability to form linkages while withholding full presence is not just an aspect of technical "things." It is an aspect of every thing, so I prefer to use the term "object" as more useful and capacious than either "stuff" or "things."

Object Humor

Humor often results when objects anticipate or exceed their in-the-moment utility. For Graham Harman, in his *Guerilla Metaphysics: Phenomenology and the Carpentry of Things*, humor requires what he calls "allure." While the normal usage of "allure" to mean "a strong attraction to something" is part of Harman's definition, he refines his usage to mean "a special and intermittent experience in which the intimate bond between a thing's unity and its plurality of notes somehow partially disintegrates."[25] For Harman, objects themselves contain many components that are subject to breaking apart. The "unity" of an object does not hold for Harman; the various elements that compose an object always exceed its wholeness. He writes, "The whole is always an oversimplification of its parts."[26] Thinking of a unified cookie jar, for instance, might obscure the materials used to craft the jar; the pigments that give the jar color and spell out the word "cookies"; the actual cookies hidden inside the jar; the flour, eggs, butter, salt, and chocolate chips that make up the cookies; the inclination of the baker to make homemade cookies; the baker's tools used in making the cookies; the desire to consume the cookies of the person who pursues the cookie jar. The parts that might connect to a cookie jar are endless; they can never be fully accounted for. The potential for breaking down, for forming something new, overrides unity. *Nancy* from April 17, 2020, illustrates Nancy's connection to a cookie jar by noting its absence when she is sick. Aunt Fritzi has left Nancy alone for twenty minutes, and readers can see a cookie jar in the background of panel 1. Panel 4 shows a close up of the cookie jar as Aunt Fritzi tells Sluggo, "The inside of that cookie jar is *somehow still full*." Fritzi knows that Nancy feels sick because she has not fallen for the allure of the cookies inside the jar. Nancy's illness has kept her from making a connection to any aspect of the cookie jar.

Harman writes, "Objects collide with each other—triggering events, forming new objects, releasing qualities into the many breezes of the world."[27] The actions that Harman describes here can come about in many ways; for my purposes, I want to focus on allure, which transforms the cookie jar and the objects to which it connects. Allure leads to humor, for Harman, "when something becomes rigid or mechanical that ought to be flexible, adaptable, appropriately mutable."[28] When the connection between the cookie jar and Nancy becomes so strong that it seems almost automatic or out of her control, her actions—or in the case of the comic above, her inaction— lead to humor. Harman writes, "What we laugh at is the way in which human . . . free decision-making power [is] undercut by . . . being delivered to the force of things, unable to master them."[29] On August 19, 2019, Fritzi warns a babysitter of the sheer force of attraction between Nancy and a cookie jar. As Fritzi and the babysitter speak in the foreground, readers see Nancy sitting at the kitchen table. The refrigerator, with a cookie jar on top, stands behind Nancy. Fritzi tells the babysitter that Nancy will eat "anything you put in front of her." Perhaps as Fritzi notices the cookie jar is behind and above Nancy, she then tells the babysitter that Nancy will eat "anything you put behind her" or "above and below her." If a cookie jar exists in any space that Nancy can access, she will find it. She cannot be stopped. Objects can overwhelm us and lead to actions that might seem out of our control. When the stakes are low, humor can result. (If the stakes were a matter of life or death, about the allure of drugs, say, rather than cookies, the result would probably not be humorous.) Jaimes's January 20, 2019, Sunday strip that opens this chapter provides a perfect illustration of how a character might be overcome by the allure of an object, in this case a cookie jar, leading to a transformation both diegetic, within the comic, and extradiegetic, in the space outside the comic on the screen and in print.

Jaimes continues playing in the boundaries between diegetic and extradiegetic spaces in later strips. For instance, her November 1, 2020, strip begins with a large rectangular panel. Anyone who has ever visited Wikipedia will recognize that this panel is a mock-Wikipedia entry, with the same layout and typeface as that website. The lines around the panel match the rest of the strip, but the content exactly matches a Wikipedia entry, as if Jaimes has cut and pasted an object into the strip. The entry panel is titled "*Nancy* 11/1/2020 strip." A redundant explanation, typical of many Wikipedia entries, follows. "**The Nancy 11/1/2020 strip** is the November 1st comic of the comic strip *Nancy*[2] from the year 2020." The first part of this sentence is in boldface to replicate the way Wikipedia emphasizes subject headings. The phrase "comic strip *Nancy*" is blue, as if it is a clickable link, and there is also what looks like a clickable footnote appended to it. Under the heading "Plot," readers are given a five-sentence summary of the strip. The rest of the strip, in four panels, appears below the Wikipedia entry. The fake entry serves as a joke on its own for technology-literate readers. The comments for this strip on GoComics show that this audience got the joke. One commenter notes that there is a "[2]" footnote without a "[1]" footnote preceding it in the entry. Another writes, "Sadly, individual comic strips do not fall under Wikipedia notability criteria for article creation." Another commenter uses Wikipedia editorial abbreviations and writes, "I propose deletion due to violations of WP:OR, WP:VENOTSUFF, and especially WP:QS." These commenters have extended the joke into the comments section, treating the strip as an actual Wikipedia entry, pointing out errors and proposing edits.

As a flexible comic creator, Jaimes provides an even more complex joke that does not depend on having a knowledge of how Wikipedia works or even what it is. The plot summary at the beginning of the strip tells us that Nancy is looking up spoilers and that Sluggo is afraid of a story's plot twists being revealed, and then in the fifth panel of the strip, he says, "All I'm scared of is being tricked into reading spoilers and having it ruin the experience for me." The strip tricks readers in exactly this way. We know what is coming in the next, final panel because we have already read the summary. Nancy's eyes glow red, and she says, "Oh . . . are you?" The strip draws readers in by doubly performing the joke about spoilers. Sluggo becomes a stand-in for the reader who fears having a plot twist spoiled, yet the plot twist has not been spoiled for Sluggo, since readers never see his reaction to Nancy's glowing red eyes. Sluggo also stands in for the reader whose experience is "ruined" by spoilers, because readers of the strip know the final plot twist before it happens. The plot reveal itself becomes the metajoke, as the reader becomes enmeshed in an ever-expanding network of reaction and commentary. As a reader and as a critic writing about comics, I feel myself drawn into the strip in a hyperaware manner. I have become part of an ever-expanding network. My enmeshment in this network echoes Coole and Frost's claim that new materialism is a "complex, pluralistic, relatively open process" of building connections with an "insistence that humans, including theorists themselves, be recognized as thoroughly immersed within materiality's productive contingencies."[30] In taking materialism seriously, one must be aware of one's status as a kind of material object. Creator, readers, fans, and critics all form part of a complex system involved in making sense of *Nancy*. Jaimes's "Wikipedia" strip pulls readers into the internet and creates more space for metahumor. Story and meaning become part of a process of reading comments and also of recognizing technological conventions of the web and of comics. Readership becomes visibly multiple in the number next to the "comment" icon next to a strip on GoComics. I know that forty-three readers reflected enough on the November 1, 2020, *Nancy* to write an online comment. Since I did not comment on it there, I should say that at least forty-four readers reflected on that strip. If you are reading this and looking at the November 1 strip, the number of reflective readers is increasing.

This multiplied readership gets reflected in *Nancy*'s content and form. On October 26, 2018, Nancy, getting ready for bed, complains to Aunt Fritzi, in the first panel of a three-panel strip, "I keep thinking I see faces in my closet at night . . . Look!" We can see the dark opening of this closet as Nancy speaks. The second panel is simply a black square, bringing readers into the space of Nancy's closet. In panel 3 Fritzi replies to

Nancy, "That's just the reflection of everybody who's reading this comic on a screen." I read this comic in print, in Jaimes's collection of the first year of strips. The black box of panel 2 was not remotely reflective. As a print reader, I could not see what Aunt Fritzi sees. But when I read the comic online, if I tilt the screen just right, I do indeed see my face reflected in the black box of the second panel. This strip literalizes the role that mediality can play in reading comic strips. Print readers are invisible in this strip, while online readers actually see their own reflection in the second panel. Jaimes uses metacomics both to make us laugh at our part in the infinite possibility of self-reflection and to render the mediations of reading as a material object. Ian Hague argues that "comics are not simply static objects that can be considered from an atemporal perspective. They change and are changed over time, modifying the space they occupy as they are being read."[31] While Hague says this is the case for all comics, contemporary flexible comics that use technological objects make the changing nature of comic reading overtly visible. Flexible comic strips themselves become a kind of media technology.

Comics as a Media Technology

Katherine Kelp-Stebbins has argued that comics, when considered as a "media technology," hold great potential for what she calls "posthuman knowledge production."[32] She writes, "The knowledge that each panel of a comic produces is contingent upon non-linear navigation between text and image and panel presentation. Panels and gutters operate as an assemblage, in networks of patterns, resonances and repetitions."[33] Jaimes's metacomics, as I discuss above, lead readers directly into such a nonlinear reading experience, as objects build connection after connection for readers to grab on to. While metacomics certainly tell us something about comics themselves, I take

Kelp-Stebbins's claim to mean that comics can tell us about much more than comics. They can work as a tool that produces knowledge that goes beyond self-reflection. For Kelp-Stebbins the term "posthuman" signifies the links—be they technological, animal, inorganic—between the human and the nonhuman. Kelp-Stebbins focuses on Jeff Lemire's graphic story *Sweet Tooth* as an exemplar of how comics can use "hybrid modes" of knowledge production and identity to produce something new, as the protagonist of the story is a human-nonhuman hybrid.

Posthuman identity draws attention to the idea that "the modes by which we recognize humanity are often founded on hierarchical binaries of self and other."[34] Breaking down these boundaries can happen on the level of character, as it does in *Sweet Tooth*. Lemire's protagonist breaks down these binaries through his very existence as he negotiates the line between human and animal so that the comics tell "us something about the relations between humanity and animality."[35] Just as important for Kelp-Stebbins, though, is the way comics, when considered as a technology, can create new ways of understanding the world. Kelp-Stebbins writes, "In *Sweet Tooth*, the boundaries between nature and culture, human and animal, man and god, and mind and body are sketchy and seamy (to say the least). Repeatedly, expectations about the diegetic world are frustrated or overturned so that the knowledge of the world it presents is always only speculative."[36] In other words, a comic like *Sweet Tooth* questions both ontological and representational boundaries. She writes, "The media technology of comics possesses an always already destabilized relation to 'reality,' necessitating renegotiations of the categories of presentation and representation."[37] Kelp-Stebbins argues that neither text nor image should be privileged "as the dominant element of comics."[38] Instead, comic scholars should embrace the hybrid nature of comics as a way of complicating signification and meaning-making. As comics exist at the border of words and images, Kelp-Stebbins claims that "comics studies cannot completely eschew the categorical boundaries in and between sign systems, yet they can call attention to the constructedness of these categories and the disciplinary discourse surrounding them."[39] In calling attention to disciplinary boundaries created by fields like literary studies and comics studies, the critic can discover something new in the interplay between text and image: "A study of comics can lay claim not simply to a different form of juxtaposing images and words in sequence, but an entirely different mode of graphiating worlds."[40] In short, comics create worlds through their unique combinations of visible objects and words. Comics occupy a space between words and images that refuses to give precedence to either. Kelp-Stebbins's configuration of comics as world-building technologies that call into question traditional boundaries seems like a particularly relevant way to think about flexible comics. She writes, "Even more, comics suggest that such distinctions may be renegotiated, especially in an increasingly multimodal media environment—just think about your desktop display."[41] Jaimes's *Nancy*, with its world of old and new objects, continually renegotiates the boundaries between page and screen, between one and multiple readers, between creator and reader. If I think of my desktop display, I think of the multiple comics I have saved to my desktop, the numerous tabs of Microsoft Word documents I have open, the number of junk emails ticking up in my inbox, the music app I have playing, my Twitter feed, the pdfs of critical essays. When I see some of these things reflected in *Nancy*, the space between diegetic and extradiegetic space blurs. I can forget where the space of the comic ends and the space of the "real" world begins.

In line with Kelp-Stebbins, thinking of comics as a media technology shows how they are a space of hybridity and possibility. Comics can make us question exactly how representation works. In this way, I want to think about comics as an aesthetic experience, especially as such experience is thought about by object-oriented ontologists Graham Harman and Timothy Morton. Harman writes that "the fate of language, as of perception and . . . of all relation, is forever to translate the dark and inward into the tangible and outward."[42] For Harman, language, perception, and relation are all forms of abstraction in that they attempt to make sense of reality in some way, whether through words, sensory experience, or connection. As noted earlier, Harman considers a world made of objects that come into contact with each other and create something new. Allure—a strong, almost mechanical, obsession—leads to humor. More generally, though, aesthetic experience is a kind of apprehension, a coming-into-contact-with that calls into question exactly how relating to something works. Harman writes that "art is granted a sort of magic power, allowing us to confront the impossible depth of objects."[43] Encountering art, or having an aesthetic experience, is a special case for object-oriented ontology. Art, be it a painting, poem, or comic strip, puts things into contact—the "us" that Harman writes of can be anybody connecting to some kind of art. Timothy Morton writes, "When you write a poem you are making a deal with some paper, some ink, word processing software, trees, editors, and air."[44] What Morton says of writing can also apply to reading, as both "reading" and "writing" in this case mean forming a network with something. What Morton calls "making a deal" is a way of thinking about materiality—all the objects he lists come together to produce something new. While this way of thinking about art might seem romantic or strangely ambiguous, it can lead to an understanding of how humor works through incongruous connections in comics.

Morton argues that aesthetic experience is "based on the capacity to be deceived" by objects.[45] Art is a kind of ambiguous lie. For this reason, art can be disturbing in the ways that it alters our understanding. Morton writes, "It's disturbing how the experience of relating to art, for example, makes it difficult—sometimes impossible—to sustain the valley across which we see other entities as 'other.' It's pretty obvious that art has an effect on me, and this effect is to a large extent unbidden: I didn't ask for it, which is part of the fun."[46] What Morton is saying here seems to me strikingly similar in content, though widely different in tone, to Kelp-Stebbins's argument about comics as a media technology that can produce new kinds of hybrid knowledge. Thinking of comics as a media technology emphasizes how they build connections and create networks; we do not read comics to see the world as it is. Instead, as Kelp-Stebbins writes, "comics do more than offer a new way of representing the world; they challenge the objective knowledge of a representable world."[47] Morton's idea that art has an effect on us that we did not ask for or even understand connects to Kelp-Stebbins's claim that comics undermine the very idea that the world can be represented through words and images. Both focus on a sort of involuntary connection. Art draws us toward it; it can disturb us when it blurs the boundary between self and other or between representation and reality. Aesthetic experience becomes its own mediality. It neither represents nor presents the world to us; instead, it breaks things down so we might lose focus as we connect with other objects, be they cookie jars, poems, or flexible metacomics.

Two of the "future" panels from the Labor Day 2018 *Nancy* strip that I discuss in chapter 1 are relevant here. One of these panels promises us Nancy on a hoverboard, holding a mobile phone on a selfie stick in one hand and a portable music device in the other and declaring, "Sluggo is lit." This panel became a popular meme and helped establish the popularity of Jaimes's *Nancy*; it was "photoshopped into various other comics and images," including Batman, the Flash, Spider-Man, the Transformers, and the "change my mind" meme.[48] In an interview, Jaimes says that this panel was "the incarnation of what I imagine my greatest hater would despise most . . . Nancy interacting with every piece of technology using words you don't understand."[49] Once again, Jaimes is thinking about how she might relate to readers and how readers might relate to *Nancy*. Jaimes overloaded Nancy with technology to antagonize her imagined critics of the comic, to tell them that they cannot relate to the humor in her new *Nancy*. Another "future" panel simply says, "Phones, phones, phones," and shows an image of a hand holding a phone with a picture of a hand holding a phone on its screen, repeated seven times as in the image becomes a *mise en abyme* of technology. There is actually a certain amount of truth to this panel, as phones appear with frequency in *Nancy*.

Representing Poochie

A series of comics where Nancy tries to capture a good image of her dog, Poochie, provides another illustration of how flexible metacomics can blur the lines between presentation and representation through media technology. With the necessary exceptions of Nancy, Sluggo, and Aunt Fritzi, Olivia Jaimes has used only two of the strip's legacy characters created during Ernie Bushmiller's long tenure on the strip: PeeWee, a small child whom Nancy sometimes babysits, and Poochie, Nancy's dog. It is worth noting that Bushmiller's representations of Poochie were inconsistent. Sometimes she had spots, sometimes she was all white, and sometimes another kid's dog looked exactly like Poochie. Legacy readers of the strip might know, then, that Poochie's appearance varied, and they might wonder how Jaimes would represent Nancy's dog. Poochie makes an unnamed brief appearance early in Jaimes's run.

She lies under a table, and Nancy rests her feet on her in the June 27, 2018, strip. She then disappears for more than a year; starting in September 2019, Poochie makes more consistent appearances in the strip.

On September 23, 2019, Jaimes teased readers who might have been wondering when Poochie would return and what she might look like. In the first panel of a four-panel strip at Nancy's school, Nancy says she wants to make her dog famous. Her teacher asks, "Since when do you have a dog, Nancy?" Nancy then describes her dog. She continues in the final panel, "She's exactly as tall as the bottom edge of every panel." Readers who wanted to see Poochie had to wait another day. Here, Jaimes created a relatable moment for legacy fans, as this strip functioned as a callout to readers who had been waiting for Poochie's return. Nancy's reference to the edge of the panel makes this strip a metacomic, as she calls our attention to the space and edges of the strip. I want to return here to Katherine Kelp-Stebbins's claim that I discuss in chapter 1—that comics "may be representations of space and spaces of representation simultaneously."[50] Poochie's invisibility illustrates how this is the case. The rectangular panels of *Nancy* mark out a "representation of space" in two ways. First, each panel delineates an exact space—panel 1 represents the space that holds Nancy and her desk, a small section of the floor, a part of the wall, and a small bit of window. The third and fourth panels draw a rectangle around a smaller space—two-thirds of Nancy's desktop, her upper body, and part of the wall behind her. Panel 2 marks out the space surrounding her teacher and her desk. Second, taking these four panels together gives us a representation of Nancy's classroom. Even if we only see Nancy at her desk in three panels and her teacher's upper body in one panel— along with the aforementioned floor, wall, and window—we "see" that these four fragments represent a larger classroom that contains more desks, students, floor, walls, and windows. We perform this kind of closure automatically; as Eszter Szép reminds us in her discussion of Scott McCloud above, we know that Nancy and her teacher are in a classroom, even as most of the classroom remains invisible to us.

Likewise, this strip can be seen as a "space of representation" in two ways. First, readers, and this writer, must bring a lot of assumptions to the act of reading to see a classroom in this strip. Most readers will have their own experience of an elementary school classroom—of desks, teachers, floors, walls, and windows. As Kelp-Stebbins writes, readers and creators "activate and mobilize these technical possibilities into emergent forms of expression and meaning."[51] Our familiarity with these objects and this spatial arrangement is something some readers might take for granted. That is, we think the elements of the strip mean "classroom," and we might take this representation of a classroom as universal. After some thought, such presuppositions reveal themselves to be false. Not every child has access to a learning space like Nancy's. Not every classroom has desks in rows and the kinds of learning technology (e.g., computers, robotic building parts) that we often see in Nancy's classroom. Being able to understand what a space means is always political, as Kelp-Stebbins claims. Seeing the space in *Nancy* as a "normal" classroom makes invisible the socioeconomic assumptions that give the students uncommented-on access to this technological space. The strip's humor appears in the second way that it works as a "space of representation." Panel 4 literally maps a space of representation as it delineates what is drawn, and thus represented to readers, from what is invisible. In this way, the panel is a frame. We can see everything inside the frame precisely because Jaimes determines the perspective and scale of the frame and controls what we can and cannot see. Jaimes could have framed the panels so that readers could see multiple desks and students or even the entire classroom. Most importantly, though, Jaimes makes the perspective represented in panel 4 "exactly" as low as Poochie's height. We would not be able to see her even if she were there. Nancy's explanation becomes a universal claim that explains Poochie's seeming absence from all previous strips (with that one earlier exception). Poochie is not just the exact right height not to fit in the panel in question, but she is also too short for "the bottom edge of every panel." With this claim, Nancy implies that Poochie could have been in *any* previous strip and been invisible to readers. Closure becomes impossible.

As in the January 20, 2019, ladder and cookie jar metacomic, Jaimes places part of Nancy's body over the border of this comic. Looking closely at the bottom line of panel 4 reveals that Nancy's thumb and part of her hand cross over the line, while the rest of her hand is just above. This hand placement creates the illusion that Nancy occupies a three-dimensional space that exists both diegetically and extradiegetically. That is, part of Nancy's hand leaves the space of panel 4 while part of it remains within the space of the panel. The panel becomes a doorway or window that can be traversed. The diegetic space below panel 4, which Nancy can see within the comic, seems to be hidden from viewers behind the opaque whiteness of the screen or newspaper where the comic strip is read. While most comics use the illusions created by lines and perspective to render their worlds three-dimensional, this particular strip (and that of the ladder and cookie jar) creates a double three-dimensional illusion, within and outside the frame of panel 4. The page itself gives depth to the frame. The self-referentiality about representation in this strip foreshadows questions of (re)presentation that surround Poochie in subsequent strips. Kelp-Stebbins has noted the "ambivalent relation of comics' (re)presentational worlds to reality."[52] Nancy's hand crossing the bottom panel line while marking the space within the frame shows just how ambivalent this relation can be.

Nancy's desire to make her dog famous involves taking pictures and videos of Poochie and posting them online. Jaimes dedicates a few strips to Nancy's attempts to take good pictures of Poochie. The October 5, 2019, strip's first panel shows Poochie sitting on the floor while Nancy looks at her phone screen, attempting to take the dog's picture. We can see a smaller image of Poochie on the phone screen, so we have two images of Poochie in the panel—a "real" Poochie sitting on the floor and a smaller "picture" of Poochie on the phone screen. Nancy says, "Poochie's so cute and funny, but I can't seem to capture it on camera . . ." What Nancy hopes to "capture" remains invisible to readers as the images are identical. In the second panel, Nancy wonders if her love for Poochie "is keeping [Nancy] from seeing her as she really is." By panel 4, Nancy reaches the conclusion that Poochie is ruining her photos as a way to get more snacks. Like the strip where readers are led to imagine Poochie just below the bottom line of any panel, this strip fails to show us some aspect of Poochie, in this case her "cuteness." Something about her continues to elude representation, and Nancy will continue looking for it. Poochie's allure, in Nancy's eyes, is unending. We see Poochie on Nancy's phone screen another time (September 25, 2019), after Nancy told her that she was "not taking the camera off her until [Nancy] was entertained . . ." Poochie sits in front of the TV, which we also see through Nancy's phone screen. Poochie makes one more appearance on Nancy's phone screen (January 24, 2020). In the first panel of this four-panel strip, when Nancy looks at her phone screen, readers can see an image of Poochie as Nancy thinks to herself that "Poochie hasn't wanted to pose for pictures lately." In panels 2 and 3 Nancy tries to sneak up on Poochie, who is lying under a table below a mirror. As the words "click click" appear in panel 4 to signify Nancy snapping a picture, we see Poochie's back leg and tail as she exits the space of the panel, leaving Nancy staring at herself in the mirror. Once again, Poochie has eluded representation. Kelp-Stebbins notes that in *Sweet Tooth* "the linework itself creates indeterminacy in representation [through] the rough-hewn and sketch-like quality of the drawings."[53] But indeterminacy can be rendered in infinite ways. Nancy's inability to take a good photo or video of Poochie illustrates how representation can fail to capture reality.

The multiple screens of the strips I have just discussed show once again how focused Jaimes is on how contemporary technology shapes our understanding of the world. In a series of comic strips where Nancy tries to train Poochie, Jaimes uses a more traditional, even old-fashioned, technique to represent Poochie: the dotted-line map. Popularized by Bill Keane's *Family Circus*, which first used it in 1962, the dotted-line map graphically shows a character's movement through a scene. In Keane's case, a dotted-line map would show Billy's rambling movements around the neighborhood as he prolonged doing a simple task. These maps are a simpler version of what Scott McCloud calls a "temporal map," or "an artists' map of time itself."[54] In other words, such a map illustrates a character's movement through time and space. On September 24, 2019, Jaimes uses a dotted-line map in a wordless four-panel strip to illustrate Nancy's failed training. The dotted lines show the multiple paths that Poochie takes to avoid jumping through a Hula-Hoop. The final panel shows an increasingly annoyed Nancy, whose facial expression turns from grin to scowl over the course of the strip. The dotted-line maps show that Poochie has been able to outsmart each of Nancy's planned routes for her. Likewise, on September 27, 2019, Jaimes uses a modified dotted-line map to show that Nancy's attempts to train Poochie are still not going well. In the first panel of this three-panel strip, Esther asks Nancy, "What are you doing with all those acorns?" In panel 2 Nancy explains that she was training Poochie to run through an obstacle course but has run out of treats. Panel 3 shows a curving line of acorns moving through the obstacle course, as Nancy says, "So I'm training all the squirrels she chases instead."

Ten days later, Nancy gives up trying to make Poochie famous. Poochie appears intermittently in future strips, usually employing a sophisticated trick to steal a treat. In that way, the Poochie strips are similar to cookie jar strips, as a character is driven to extremes by desire for a food item. In the case of the strips where Nancy attempts to train Poochie, the desire to achieve something is doubled. Poochie's desire for a treat always beats out Nancy's desire to train her. Jaimes's use of Poochie works for multiple audiences, showing Jaimes's flexibility in creating humor in different ways. She connects Poochie to the new objects of phones and screens to produce humorous metacomics about representation itself. And she uses the old objects of dog treats and dotted-line maps to produce humorous strips about Nancy's thwarted ambition and Poochie's intelligence.

Throughout her run on the strip, Jaimes has used flexible humor by combining and switching between the new and the old. Even her humorous use of twenty-first-century objects like Snapchat filters harkens back to Nancy's material history as a legacy comic. In *How to Read "Nancy,"* Newgarden and Karasik provide an anatomy of formal techniques Ernie Bushmiller used to produce jokes. One section emphasizes "the inked line"—as they write, "In comics, all is ultimately expressed through line."[55] One of the examples they use to illustrate this point is a Bushmiller strip from November 23, 1944. The first panel shows a drawing board with a half-finished comic on it and a desk with an inkwell on the right side of the panel. In the unfinished comic, Nancy tells Sluggo that she wishes "he'd finish this strip" so they can do something else. Sluggo replies that "he ate too much toikey and he fell asleep." In the second panel of the unfinished strip, Sluggo takes up the pen we saw in panel 1 and finishes the strip. The final panel then frames the completed strip-within-a-strip, with a very poorly drawn Nancy and Sluggo saying, "Happy Thanksgiving everybody." Badly drawn lines in this strip serve the same purpose as those in Jaimes's April 16, 2018, Snapchat filter strip discussed at the beginning of the chapter. How each creator makes these poorly drawn lines reflects the technologies of their times: Bushmiller's pen, ink, and paper; Jaimes's screen and digital drawing tools.

Likewise, Bushmiller often drew strips that showed Poochie avoiding obstacles and outsmarting Nancy to get food. He even used Poochie in a holiday metacomic. On April 1, 1950, Nancy looks at the calendar and, realizing it is April Fool's Day, says that nobody will play a trick on her. She takes Poochie for a walk. Panel 3 shows an off-panel voice saying, "Is that so?" As the right side of the panel shows a hand holding a pen, the left side of the panel shows us that the artist has switched Nancy's and Poochie's heads. Once again, metacomics are rooted in their days' objects: pen and ink for Bushmiller and screens for Jaimes's metacomics on Poochie. While Bushmiller's and Jaimes's metacomics share similarities, the historical specificity of the objects in their respective strips illustrate different ways of making a joke. Bushmiller's metajokes rely on his control of his characters. He can use the power of his pen to switch characters' heads or to take a day off from work (as he does in his Labor Day strips). Jaimes's metajokes, and more generally her humor, focus more on her confidence in her drawing technique and her questioning of how computer technology affects representation. Metacomics date back to the creation of comic strips, but that does not mean that their jokes are not rooted in specific technologies and cultural concerns.

In my final chapter, I turn to how Jaimes uses the technological objects of the twenty-first century as she explores how the coronavirus pandemic affects her characters and readers. Jaimes never mentions COVID-19 by name. Instead, she uses objects—masks, hand sanitizer bottles, video-chat boxes, and webcam images—to show how Nancy and her friends adapt to the technologies that the pandemic has made familiar to the students, teachers, and workers who have access to the same safety measures that Nancy and her cohorts do. As I have argued throughout this book, Jaimes's *Nancy* exists in a strongly mediated world of technology. As such, the strip is uniquely equipped to illustrate how remote learning creates new subjectivities that were hard to envision even a few years ago. Jaimes's response to the pandemic shows that daily flexible comics can make visible some of the ways that the world changes around us. Jaimes's use of pandemic iconography makes the strip relatable in specific ways, while highlighting some of the problematic aspects that link visuality and surveillance in the real world.

5. *Nancy*, by Olivia Jaimes, November 3, 2020. NANCY © 2020. Reprinted by permission of ANDREWS MCMEEL SYNDICATION for UFS. All rights reserved.

4

"You've Got Your Mask, Right?"

Nancy's Pandemic (November 3, 2020)

Moving School Online

Olivia Jaimes includes Election Day in the pantheon of holidays and special events that mark time every year in the strip: Christmas, New Year's, Nancy's birthday, April Fool's Day, the last day of school, Labor Day, the first day of school, Halloween, and Thanksgiving. On November 3, 2020, Aunt Fritzi tells Nancy that she's going to vote at her school. Fritzi says, "It's like we've switched places," since Nancy's classes have been online. Nancy replies, "Like *that* would ever happen." In the final panel, we see Nancy's phone screen doubling the image of Fritzi standing at the door with her backpack on. The image on Nancy's screen makes Fritzi look child sized, as if they have indeed switched places. This Election Day strip marks the first time that *Nancy* refers to masks. None of Jaimes's characters have been portrayed as wearing masks up to this point. Nancy's question, then, becomes an acknowledgement that people in the real world, and in the world of the strip, are wearing masks to curtail spread of the coronavirus.

Fritzi's comment that Nancy's classes have been online all year points to the strip's clearest references to events in the real world, from April 2020. On April 11, 2020, Nancy reads a message on her laptop that says, "Robot tournament canceled for rest of year." On April 13 a librarian tells Sluggo that the "library's closed for now, kid." And on April 22 Nancy logs on to class online for the first time. It is not until March 17, 2021, that Nancy says, "In-person school is happening again." None of these comics say why events have been canceled, libraries closed, and school moved online. Anyone experiencing similar occurrences in the real world during this time could assume that the strip was referring to the COVID-19 pandemic. The choices that Jaimes makes in creating strips about the pandemic point to a time conundrum that all daily comic strips face. While time passes over the course of a year in daily comics, characters rarely age. Nancy perpetually turns nine every March 15. At the same time, *Nancy* clearly takes place in a twenty-first-century world of mobile phones, laptop computers, and social media. Therefore, like most other daily strips, *Nancy* exists in a space where time repeats in a yearly cycle and a space where its objects locate it in a specific time period. While *Nancy* never mentions the pandemic directly, readers can obviously see that the strip has been responding to it. Even if Nancy will perpetually be in the fourth grade, readers will know that nearly a year of Nancy's schooling took place remotely. Daily comics exist in a kind of time paradox. Most daily comic strips follow "comic strip time," where characters do not age or radically change. At the same time, many daily comics represent real-world events and changing technologies.

Even without the differences between the ways time passes in a strip and in the real world, daily comic creators face difficult choices in writing about current events. A 2021 article about how comic creators make such decisions notes the multiple temporal questions they must address: "Unlike internet cartoonists, who can respond immediately to current events, creators of daily newspaper strips work about two weeks in advance, sometimes longer."[1] Sunday comics have an even longer lead time, and some creators work months in advance. For instance,

Stephen Pastis, creator of *Pearls before Swine*, usually works nine months ahead of time.[2] Despite these constraints that make it difficult to respond in a timely manner to ever-changing events (such as how different states enacted lockdowns and mask mandates), many creators decided to address the pandemic, often putting aside strips they had already created. Pastis has said he wants comics to remain "relevant," noting, "I can't think of another time when every single person was thinking of the exact same thing, and if you're not reflecting that, what are you doing?"[3] Thus, he directly addresses quarantines, mask wearing, and social distancing on an almost daily basis in his strip. When he decided to write about the pandemic, Pastis had to shelve months of already finished strips. On the other hand, Sandra Bell-Lundy, creator of *Between Friends*, decided not to address the pandemic, for multiple reasons. She worried that it would be impossible to resolve a narrative arc centered on the pandemic, because "it looks like this is going to be for another year, maybe even two."[4] *Between Friends* takes place mainly in an office, and Bell-Lundy noted that her characters would not be able to interact at work: "The writing would just be too limited" if her characters all worked from home and only interacted via video chat.[5] Video chats, though, have been a part of *Nancy* since Jaimes's reboot. Jaimes's strip has always focused on the ways that screens affect her characters' lives; their moving to wholly online communication in school, work, and friendship was more of a shift in degree than in kind for *Nancy*. As discussed in the previous chapter, *Nancy*, as a flexible daily comic, enmeshes itself in a self-referential network of media technologies. Nancy, Sluggo, Fritzi, and friends have always been technologically mediated subjects. As the real world has come to rely increasingly on online communication technologies during the pandemic, it has become increasingly like the world of *Nancy*.

Nancy's school moves online in spring 2020 and stays online through the fall. Summer robotics club likewise becomes virtual. From April 17 through the end of June, characters mostly interact in person with others who live in in the same household. Sluggo conveniently stays with Nancy and Fritzi, as his uncles with whom he lives work "on the road." (These uncles have never appeared in the strip, and Sluggo's homelife is rarely discussed.) Twin sisters Agnes and Lucy interact at home, and Jaimes shows readers more of Esther's life at home. We learn that Esther lives with her older sister and that she has a pet chameleon. In their various households, the kids confront their boredom. Sluggo briefly takes up whittling, Nancy and Fritzi work on jigsaw puzzles, Agnes and Lucy draw, and Esther plays basketball by herself. All these pursuits will be relatable to those in Jaimes's audience who confronted pandemic boredom, as will the amount of time everyone in the strip spends online for those audience members who have regular internet access. Most of the strips that focus on school, from April 2020 until March 2021, focus on video chats.

Jaimes shows the relatable frustrations of this technology through one of Nancy's teachers, Melissa Bangles. On April 22 her speech balloon is blank as she attempts to speak to Nancy via computer. Nancy tells her twice that she is muted. In the final panel, the teacher has turned on another microphone that creates audio feedback. Jaimes visually represents this with overlapping images of the fourth panel, which shows Nancy looking at her teacher on-screen, as the teacher asks what's wrong with a little "feedback." The word "feedback" is nearly illegible as Jaimes places numerous slightly overlapping repetitions of the word on the page, just as aural feedback repeats soundwaves and makes them inaudible. In a two-panel strip on April 23, Nancy tells Sluggo that students have to watch their teachers closely in online classes. The second panel shows a close-up of Bangles on Nancy's laptop screen, with an image of a cat reflected on the lenses of her glasses. Nancy tells Sluggo, "You can tell when she's not paying attention by the memes reflected in her glasses." On the last day of classes (June 24, 2020), Bangles ends the class meeting and hangs up. In panel 2 she raises her hands in celebration as she says, "I'm free!" Panel 3 shows Nancy and Sluggo looking quizzically at their laptop screen as they hear their teacher say that "she finally mastered the video chat controls." In the final panel, she says, "I was really starting to get the kids' respect by being cool and aloof," as Nancy and Sluggo stare at their screen, where a small image of their teacher shares the screen with the question, "Are you sure you want to end this meeting?" Notably, this teacher and Aunt Fritzi, who complains to Nancy of a sore neck on October 1, 2020, because "I always forget to look up and stretch when I'm staring down at the computer all day," are the only characters frustrated by videoconferencing. Nancy and her friends adapt without complaint.

Manipulating Technology

Nancy, instead, continually manipulates computer technology to avoid work. On May 28, 2020, she moves the angle of her screen so her "teacher can't see me playing video games during class." Sluggo moves his screen so that his computer camera gives the teacher a view of Nancy. On July 29, 2020, her teacher gives the class an on-screen puzzle to "use the small shapes to make the big shape." Not wanting anyone to see her making an effort, Nancy thinks to herself that she will block everyone's view by making an obstruction in front of her camera. She manipulates rectangular books, triangular sandwich halves, and a notebook as she attempts to build the obstruction, which winds up looking just like the puzzle image on her screen. On September 25, 2020, when Nancy has difficulty with a math problem, she doesn't want the rest of the class to think "I'm *trying too hard.*" She decides to "pretend to be done by striking a casual pose." She puts on a pair of sunglasses and picks up a skateboard as she says to the computer camera, "That problem was a total breeze." Nancy almost obsessively tries to find ways to distort what her camera shows others. For her, online class is all about the image that her camera shows her classmates and teacher. When Nancy and Agnes meet up in person in the summer (June 26, 2020), Nancy says that she's glad to talk to someone in person but that she's "still adjusting to not seeing a tiny version of myself in the corner when we talk." Agnes tells her that she's still looking at herself as they talk in person. We then see Nancy looking at her reflection in a store window, saying that now she is seeing "a big version of myself." Nancy's teacher even tricks Nancy into paying attention in science class by showing a slide of "the inside of a plant cell and Nancy's yearbook photo from last year" (September 14, 2020). The final panel of this strip is visually complex. On the left quarter of a double-sized panel, a tall rectangle shows Nancy's teacher speaking. The middle of the panel shows the top and bottom lines of the slide, with a picture of the plant cell next to a small rectangle showing Nancy's yearbook photo. The right side of the panel shows three stacked rectangles, connected by small lines, showing, from the bottom up, Agnes, Sluggo, and a smiling Nancy, who is clearly pleased to see her yearbook image on screen. This layered image of seven rectangles in one panel is remarkably easy to read for anyone familiar with the look of videoconferencing interfaces, which is likely most of Jaimes's audience. Even in 2019 this panel might have seemed less legible to many readers. With its lines and rectangles within rectangles, it looks like an attempt at representing a complex passing of time. Instead, it represents a simple moment of action on a computer screen.

Jaimes uses a simple visual language to represent both an adult frustration with technology and Nancy's fascination with the images it produces. The rectangles of screens, and the rectangles within those rectangles that show faces, may have become more relatable to readers who had the ability to learn and work remotely as the pandemic progressed. In representing screens so frequently, Jaimes has drawn attention to the materiality of the actual comic strip. The chat boxes and boxed-in faces of videoconferencing resemble comic strip panels. Both create an illusion of depth on a flat surface, and both reduce representation to two dimensions. The line between *Nancy* and the world it represents is a thin one.

Politics and Daily Comics

Of course, daily comic strips rarely directly address catastrophic events like the illness and death the world has seen from COVID-19. After interviewing numerous comic creators about their response to the pandemic, Josh Fruhlinger concludes that they all "seemed hesitant to integrate the disease itself, as opposed to the overall social changes that have arisen from its spread, into their strips."[6] Part of the reason for this reluctance might be simply that daily newspaper comics are, in Fruhlinger's words, an "incredibly ephemeral medium" read on their day of publication and then forgotten by most readers.[7] Fruhlinger also notes that many daily comic creators see their strips as a kind of "escapist fantasy" for readers who do not want to face the news of the day on the comic page.[8] For such creators, readers can easily turn to the news section of the paper to read about reality.

Likewise, most daily comic creators do not engage in direct political commentary, like referring to specific office holders or legislation. Those daily comics that do offer commentary on contemporary politics—such as Walt Kelly's *Pogo*, Garry

Trudeau's *Doonesbury*, Aaron McGruder's *The Boondocks*, and Bruce Tinsley's *Mallard Fillmore*—have faced the possibilities of being moved to the editorial page or removed from the comic page. In "Censorship on the Comics Page: Walt Kelly's 'Pogo' and American Political Culture in the Cold War Era," Eric Jarvis writes that *Pogo* occasionally led newspaper editors to "control or mute the political satire" in the strip when Kelly directly addressed four issues in the 1950s and '60s: McCarthyism, Communism, southern racial segregation, and the Vietnam War.[9] Three tactics were used by editors to censor *Pogo*. They sometimes directly altered or deleted certain aspects of the strips; other times, editors decided to take "the more drastic step of dropping the strip entirely for a time." At other times, editors moved "politically inspired installments . . . out of the comics section and into the editorial pages."[10] In the 1960s Kelly even drew alternate strips for overtly political ones that editors might not want to print. Kelly dubbed these strips "bunny rabbit strips," because they featured his regular cast of swamp creatures and no political commentary.[11] Meanwhile, Garry Trudeau's *Doonesbury* has, since the 1970s, directly referred to specific politicians and sociopolitical issues. Newspaper editors have moved numerous *Doonesbury* strips to the editorial pages, from those about Watergate in 1973 to strips about Bill Clinton's impeachment in 1993.[12] Trudeau has preferred to call such choices "editing" and not censorship; he has said, "I have never presumed that with the wide range of community standards and editorial constraints that exist within the newspaper community that I would or should be welcome in every client paper on every day."[13] When Aaron McGruder criticized "post-9/11 media coverage . . . and the federal government" in October 2001, "it was soon pulled from the funny pages of at least three newspapers."[14] More recently, Gannett newspaper publications permanently dropped *Mallard Fillmore* from its newspapers because the strip "did not meet our standards," after two strips criticized Joe Biden's stances on climate change and transgender athletes.[15]

Of course, the COVID-19 pandemic has been politicized in the United States. Daily newspaper comics rarely focus on the political ramifications of mask wearing or vaccine mandates. Rather, as Fruhlinger notes above, creators tend to pay more attention to the social aspects of the pandemic.[16] Webcomic creators, who do not face the lag time between writing and publication of newspaper comic creators, have published comics that cover a broad range of pandemic-focused topics. The Graphic Medicine website (graphicmedicine.org) has compiled hundreds of COVID-19 comics. In their article "Comics in the Time of a Pan(dem)ic: COVID-19, Graphic Medicine, and Metaphors," Sweetha Saji, Sathyaraj Venkatesan, and Brian Callender coin the term "covidity" to explain what these comics do. They write, "Covidity embraces wide-ranging individual and collective responses/reactions . . . including the need to reinvent oneself in the context of constant disruption, and the trauma of everyday life. The assumption is that in an unprecedented crisis, an individual develops an idiosyncratic philosophical attitude towards one-self and to others, *often engendering a distinctive subjectivity*" (emphasis added).[17] While the comics that Saji and colleagues consider directly address the pandemic in ways that *Nancy* and other daily flexible comics do not, I claim that *Nancy* pays close attention to the "distinctive subjectivity" created by the pandemic. As I have been arguing throughout this book, *Nancy* has a strongly self-aware focus on technologically mediated subjectivity. Because of this focus, the strip cannot help but address the ways that the pandemic has altered its cast's ways of living in the world. In a short article in the *Lancet* about COVID-19 comics, Brian Callender, Shirlene Obuobi, M. K. Czerwiec, and Ian Williams write about the specific ways that comics can approach the pandemic. They write, "Comics can depict and articulate spatial, temporal, and relational aspects of the pandemic in ways that may be more challenging for other media to portray. . . . Comics can delineate the social, bodily, and geographical boundaries that have been impacted by the virus, the reconfiguring of social interactions, and emotional responses to such things as physical distancing, isolation, and the risk of becoming infected."[18] While *Nancy* does not directly confront medical issues, it certainly says a lot about the social and emotional impact of the pandemic. Callender and colleagues write that "invisibility is an important aspect of contagion. Both the viral pathogen and the routes of transmission cannot be seen by the naked eye."[19] For them, COVID-19 comics can render visible the "unseen clinical spaces where the physical and emotional toll of the pandemic weighs heavily."[20] *Nancy* serves a similar purpose in making visible the social effects of the pandemic in everyday life.

Online Visibility and the Spread of Surveillance

In Jaimes's *Nancy*, technology grounds the strip in a specific time. In an interview, Jaimes says that she wants "the strip to always match the time period in which it's occurring." Technology plays a big role in representing a specific period of time. As Jaimes says, "Ten years ago, I didn't have a smartphone and my life was very different. And I'm thinking, ten years in the future, if that's the way things continue to grow, there are gonna be totally new annoyances related to technology that Nancy has to deal with or whine about."[21] At the time of this interview (2019), Jaimes could not have anticipated that a pandemic would reinforce our reliance on screens. Jaimes could, however, anticipate that technology always creates new ways to intervene in our lives. As more of her life moved online, Nancy responded as she always had, by complaining and by thinking of novel ways to subvert the rules that govern her. When these rules began to be delivered via online tools, Nancy embraced that technology to undermine her teachers' authority. What becomes a "new annoyance" for Nancy is how her teachers' roles have expanded beyond the classroom and into her home. Nancy must now contend with the robotics kit that her teacher sends to her home when robotics club is canceled. When she receives the kit, Nancy says, "I'm not going to be duped into spending my free time building something with this" (December 5, 2020). Instead, she uses the box that holds the kit as a step stool to get closer to the cookie jar that sits on top of the refrigerator. Likewise, Nancy realizes that remote schooling means that she won't get a snow day when it is snowing outside (December 1, 2020). When Fritzi tells her that snow days "are about safety" and that she can reach her computer simply by getting out of bed, Nancy throws banana peels on her bedroom floor to increase the risk of safely reaching her computer.

Nancy, while schooling at home, resists the incursion of authority into the space of her bedroom. In her 2019 essay, "E(a)ffective Precarity, Control and Resistance in the Digitalised Workplace," Phoebe V. Moore argues that increasingly online work is leading toward a greater control over previously private aspects of people's lives. She writes that "the trend in uses of technology to control areas of unseen labour through newly digitalised workplaces, with the use of location and sensory devices that threaten to capture and control our every movement, sentiment and thought, [blurs] the categories between work and life themselves."[22] While the tone of *Nancy* remains lighthearted, the ways that technology infiltrates Nancy's private time and space echo the workplace concerns that Moore writes about. Moore examines the "everyday forms of resistance to this invasive level of control" that workers engage in, where "people may 'steal' breaks and mask them as work; or simply

[drag] their feet" or take actions like sabotage and "chronic absenteeism."[23] Such resistance becomes one means by which "people find dignity and self-worth within labour."[24] Nancy's motivations might be configured differently—she sees herself embracing laziness as its own end rather than as a means of finding dignity at work—but Nancy's resistance to the surveillance of remote learning resonates with the forms of resistance that workers might employ in relation to digital surveillance. As shown in earlier chapters, Jaimes's strip continually reflects on the precarity at the heart of contemporary comic creation. *Nancy* cannot help but relate to the ways that technology is deployed in our world, in both the workplace and the classroom.

As the pandemic forced many colleges and universities into remote learning, online surveillance of students increased immensely. Exam-monitoring corporations like Proctorio, ProctorU, and Respondus Monitor saw rising demand for their products. Proctorio claims that "its software administered an estimated twenty-one million exams in 2020, compared with four million in 2019."[25] Surveillance proctoring has raised pedagogical, privacy, and fairness issues, as some professors and students question the invasiveness of this technology. The kinds of student subjects created through interactions with proctoring software resonate with the online subjectivities that Jaimes creates in *Nancy*. While the stakes are low in Nancy's online interaction with her teachers (as she mostly schemes to avoid work), college students face serious consequences in their interactions with online proctoring. Nonetheless, Nancy's manipulation of how her teachers and classmates see her webcam image shares striking similarities with the machinations that surveilled students are forced to go through as schools attempt to keep them from cheating on exams.

Most proctoring software requires students to upload a webcam picture of themselves and to pan their webcam around their room to prove their identity and to show that no one is in the room feeding them answers. A Black student at the University of Texas at Austin, Femi Yemi-Ese, had difficulty getting Proctorio's software to recognize his facial image via a webcam photo. Without this recognition, the software would not let him access the exam. The software's seeming ability to only recognize lighter-skinned faces shows how visibility and racism can intersect. Yemi-Ese had to turn on brighter lighting in his room and tilt "his camera to catch his face at its most illuminated angle; it took several tries before the software approved him to begin."[26] Online-monitoring programs also note students' eye movements. If the software determines that students look away from their computer monitor too often, it will flag the behavior as suspicious. Students like Yemi-Ese are forced into absurd situations. The combination of the bright lighting needed for facial recognition and the requirement to keep one's eyes looking toward a webcam compounds the difficulty of test taking. Yemi-Ese explains that he had to "have a light beaming into my eyes for the entire exam. . . . That's hard when you're actively trying not to look away, which could make it look like you're cheating."[27] Another student faced losing her scholarship after ProctorU reported to her professor that she had exhibited suspicious behavior while taking an exam. This student posted her experiences on TikTok under the name @_.daynuh._. ProctorU software flagged her for possible cheating because the webcam recording of the student showed her reading one of the exam questions aloud, as if she were reading the question to another person outside the view of the webcam. The student explains, "I was just rereading the question, so I could better understand it."[28] Despite her B grade on the exam, the student's professor gave her an F for cheating. Only after appealing to the dean of students and acquiring from ProctorU a copy of the video of her taking the exam was the student able to convince the professor to reinstate her passing grade. These two examples illustrate that test-taking college students subjected to this kind of surveillance technology must alter their behavior in specific ways (e.g., keeping their eyes on screen and not talking) to avoid being flagged for suspicious behavior.[29]

As discussed throughout this book, Jaimes uses *Nancy* to explore the social and cultural ramifications of technology-mediated subjectivity. Students subjected to online proctoring software live in a world that is strongly relatable to Nancy's, as they must continually negotiate their self-presentation through webcam-mediated surveillance. The stakes are of course much lower for Nancy's negotiations. She wants to be lazy and do as little work as possible, while real-world students face much more serious consequences. The real-world examples that I cite above show the risks of online subjectivity for students who do not or cannot follow the norms instantiated by proctoring software. Facial recognition software is much more likely to "misidentify Asian and Black faces than they are white ones."[30] Students with disabilities worry that proctoring software will flag as suspicious such behaviors as resizing typeface and altering their computer monitor's color scheme to make text more legible.[31] More broadly, students must worry about whether online proctoring constitutes "an excessive invasion of privacy and jeopardization of students' personal information and data."[32] The relative simplicity of showing up to a classroom to take an exam has been replaced by a complex system of mediation that has little to do with the student learning that tests are supposed to measure.

The CEO of Proctorio, Mike Olsen, "said that his company could hold on to its COVID-era gains by presenting itself as a flexible, inexpensive alternative to traditional testing venues."[33] I discuss in my introduction how comics must become flexible to survive in the contemporary world by negotiating questions of labor, readership, cultural identity, and technology. While *Nancy* often portrays this flexibility in a humorous way, the very act of making flexibility visible serves to connect the comic to real-world concerns about the risks of flexibility, even as these risks do not exist in *Nancy*'s world. Olsen says that "for us, as a company, it's an opportunity" to grow the use of proctoring software.[34] Those subject to the software are left to ask what this opportunity might cost them.

Some students have responded to online proctoring in a very Nancy-like manner, by gaming the system and finding ways to cheat that the software cannot measure, according to an article published on Vice. Just as Nancy shows a strong awareness of what is inside and outside the frame of her webcam and just as Jaimes plays with the spaces that are internal and external to the frames of her comic strip (see, as one example, the previous chapter's discussion of Poochie's existence outside the panel's frame), exam-taking students have "spread sheets of notes on the floor" and "printed out . . . notes using a large font and stuck them to the wall . . . out of view" of the teacher.[35] By taking advantage of the space that exists outside the frame of their webcams, these students have negotiated a spatial world similar to Nancy's, a world where the line between what is inside and outside the frame is of the utmost importance. More technologically savvy students have taken advantage of the fact that a computer's keyboard is out of the webcam's frame. One student, interviewed by Vice, developed a plan that reads like an idea that Nancy would be proud to emulate. The student said, "My friend put a phone on a stand on his keyboard so it couldn't be seen during the room and desk sweep. . . . Then we FaceTimed with me at the other end. . . . The phone was at a slant so he could see me and I could see the exam. Then I would just hold up a flashcard with a, b, c, or d."[36] All the students interviewed assured the interviewer that they had not been caught. Their ability to adapt to the incursions of surveillance technology resonates through the world of Jaimes's strip.

It is important to emphasize that Nancy is a fictional nine-year-old girl and not a gig worker or college student subject to the real-world risks of pandemic-enabled surveillance technology. Nancy's ways of interacting with technology involve both resistance and acceptance. While she continually tries to undermine the learning process of online school, she also embraces many of the aspects of living online. On March 15, 2021, Nancy happily holds her birthday party virtually. In each of the strip's three panels, Nancy repeats how great it is that her friends are "*virtual*," as they watch her slide a whole cake onto her plate and as they hear her eating. Nancy says that she is glad her friends are "here . . . , but not *here*-here"; that is, since they are not in the same physical space, Nancy can finally achieve her goal of hogging all the snacks. Her friends can only stare at their cameras as Nancy eats.

Mediated Time and Space

When Nancy returns to school at the end of March, she complains about the social-distancing rules that prevent her from passing notes to Esther as "yet another way modern life has drained our childhood of all fun and whimsy" (March 23, 2021). This strip marks the first time that Jaimes has drawn Nancy and Esther wearing masks. These masks serve as a means of representing "modern life" in 2021. Nancy's world is the world of the pandemic. Even as Jaimes acknowledges the objects that represent the pandemic, Nancy uses these objects in new ways. At the end of the strip, she uses a mask as a slingshot to shoot a note across the room to Esther. A day earlier, Nancy squirts hand sanitizer all over her homework and then tells her friend that Fritzi yelled at her "for being **too** sanitary" (March 22, 2021). On March 29, 2021, Nancy complains, via video chat, to her grandmother, that she is no longer allowed to sit in the "amazing seat" that she had picked out at the beginning of the school year, as we see Aunt Fritzi drag Nancy away from her bed where her laptop sits. As Nancy returns to in-person school, she adapts to her times. On March 30, 2021, readers see Nancy and her teacher in the classroom. Both are masked as the teacher talks about their "hybrid school schedule." For the rest of the school year, Nancy and her classmates wear masks and have laptop computers on their desks.

Jaimes also returns to story lines that had to be altered because of the pandemic. Nancy tells Sluggo on May 15, 2021, that the library has reopened and that he can become "a huge secret nerd again," picking up the story of Sluggo's reading in the library that had been paused in April 2020 when the library closed. Over the next few strips, we see a masked Sluggo secretly reading while the mask-wearing librarians chat. Outside of the classroom and the library, Jaimes does not draw any characters wearing masks.

Yet *Nancy*'s times cannot help but be a little out of sync with the real world. As the pandemic continued into the late summer of 2021, Jaimes focused less on the pandemic. A large number of summer 2021 strips centered on Nancy's scheme to help the robotics team. Her plan makes the team lose a competition, and Nancy's teammates are once again angry at her. Through July and August 2021, Nancy tries to make up with Esther and the other members of the club. While the details of their falling out are different, this story line clearly echoes the argument and subsequent reconciliation between Nancy and Esther that developed from January through July 2019 (discussed in chapter 2). As "comic strip time" continually circles back to the same milestones year after year while the characters remain the same age, it also allows for the recurrence of plots. Nancy and Esther may continue to put their friendship in jeopardy because of robotics club year after year, just as they may reconcile again and again. Paradoxically, "comics time" also allows for remembrance of past events. On June 15, 2021, Esther thinks that robotics club was more fun when Nancy was in it. We then see four panels under the heading "Flashback Time" that show Esther's memories of building a robot with Nancy. Even as the characters live through recurring events, the strip has made a few recent oblique references to changing aspects of the pandemic that connect their world to real time. On July 29, 2021, Nancy worries about leaving Poochie alone "now that we're leaving the house again after being home so often." Readers can clearly take this as a reference to the optimism in the United States that the pandemic was nearing its end as the summer progressed. The July and August 2021 surge in cases due to the delta variant of the virus make this strip seem a bit out of time. The contentious debates about mask wearing, social distancing, and vaccination mandates that happened at the beginning of the 2021–22 school year seem foreign to Nancy's comic strip world.

Well after the publication of these 2021 strips, our understanding of and reaction to the pandemic will undoubtedly be different. Daily newspaper comics will always be weeks or months behind in their response to changing events. Nevertheless, flexible daily comics like *Nancy* will continue to make visible in two dimensions, on our screens and in our newspapers, how we always live in mediated time and space.

NOTES

INTRODUCTION. "GOING *IN* ON THAT CORNBREAD"

1. Ian Gordon's in-depth *Comic Strips and Consumer Culture, 1890–1945* details a time period when newspaper comics were at the height of their cultural capital.

2. While the days of the "star" creator have mostly passed in newspaper comics, they live on in graphic novels and superhero comics. Graphic novel stars like Alison Bechdel and Chris Ware have no real equivalents in daily comic strips. Likewise, superhero writers and artists like Tom King, Gail Simone, and Brian Stelfreeze can sell comics on their name alone. Other star creators like Kelly Sue DeConnick and Kieron Gillen write both superhero comics and independent comics. Daily comic strips rarely have creators who have gained fame elsewhere, while Marvel and DC often hire well-known filmmakers, novelists, and essayists such as Reginald Hudlin, Kevin Smith, Nnedi Okorafor, Ta-Nehisi Coates, and Roxane Gay.

3. Grieco, "Fast Facts."

4. Hatfield, *Alternative Comics*, 2–3.

5. Hatfield, *Alternative Comics*, 3.

6. Both sites offer premium memberships, comment sections, and other ways for fans to engage with comics.

7. Kashtan, *Between Pen and Pixel*, 3.

8. Walker, *Comics*, 354.

9. The contracts signed by syndicated comic creators stand in strong contrast to the work-for-hire model that comic book artists were forced to work under. Bart Beaty, in *Comics versus Art*, writes that Jack Kirby "was paid a flat page rate for his work and nothing else," even as characters he created and cocreated "have generated billions of dollars in revenue" for Marvel and DC (88). Beaty contrasts the earnings of comic book artists with the "great financial success" achieved by Charles Schulz, to highlight how different working conditions were between comic book artists and syndicated comic strip creators.

10. Gateward and Jennings, "Introduction," 9.

11. Goldstein, "Fashion in the Funny Papers," 109.

12. Howard and Jackson, introduction, 20.
13. Goldstein, "The Trouble with Romance," 57.
14. Goldstein, "The Trouble with Romance," 52.
15. Goldstein, "The Trouble with Romance," 55.
16. Goldstein, "The Trouble with Romance," 57.
17. Heer, afterword, 431.
18. Heer, afterword, 431.
19. Karasik and Newgarden, *How to Read "Nancy,"* 52.
20. Karasik and Newgarden, *How to Read "Nancy,"* 53–54.
21. Karasik and Newgarden, *How to Read "Nancy,"* 34, ellipses in original.
22. Karasik and Newgarden, *How to Read "Nancy,"* 52.
23. Karasik and Newgarden, *How to Read "Nancy,"* 52.
24. Watterson and Robb, *Exploring "Calvin and Hobbes,"* 38.
25. Watterson and Robb, *Exploring "Calvin and Hobbes,"* 38.
26. Cavna, "'Nancy' and Artist Olivia Jaimes."
27. Jaimes, "Olivia Jaimes, the Mysterious Cartoonist," 124.
28. Cavna, "For the First Time."
29. Jaimes, "Olivia Jaimes, the Mysterious Cartoonist," 124.
30. Cavna, "'Nancy' and Artist Olivia Jaimes."
31. Cavna, "'Nancy' and Artist Olivia Jaimes."
32. Cavna, "'Nancy' and Artist Olivia Jaimes."
33. Andersen, "*Sarah's Scribbles.*"
34. Kleefeld, *Webcomics*, 114.
35. Kleefeld, *Webcomics*, 114.
36. Ross, *Nice Work If You Can Get It*, 2–3.
37. Kleefeld, *Webcomics*, 58.
38. Kleefeld, *Webcomics*, 58. The comics.com domain was eventually bought out and absorbed by the website GoComics.
39. Priego, "On Cultural Materialism," 2.
40. Priego, "On Cultural Materialism," 2.
41. Hatfield, *Alternative Comics*, 58.
42. Hatfield, *Alternative Comics*, 58.
43. Szép, *Comics and the Body*, 163.
44. Kashtan, *Between Pen and Pixel*, 6.
45. Kashtan, *Between Pen and Pixel*, 23.
46. Jenkins, *Comics and Stuff*, 2.
47. Jenkins, *Comics and Stuff*, 22.
48. Jenkins, *Comics and Stuff*, 23.
49. Jenkins, *Comics and Stuff*, 29.
50. Szép, *Comics and the Body*, 5.

51. Szép, *Comics and the Body*, 5.
52. Szép, *Comics and the Body*, 24–25.
53. Hague, *Comics and the Senses*, 7.
54. Hague, *Comics and the Senses*, 23.
55. I do not mean to imply that Szép's and Hague's theorizations of embodied materiality are the same. For important ways that their respective ideas differ, see Szép's *Comics and the Body*, 22–23, 141–42.
56. Brown, "Survival at Work," 721.
57. Priego, "On Cultural Materialism," 2.
58. Priego, "On Cultural Materialism," 2.
59. Gordon, *Comic Strips and Consumer Culture*, 14.
60. Gordon, *Comic Strips and Consumer Culture*, 14.
61. Harman, *Object-Oriented Ontology*, 54.
62. Bartosch, "Understanding Comics' Mediality," 243.
63. Bartosch, "Understanding Comics' Mediality," 245.
64. See also Katherine Kelp-Stebbins's work, especially her "Hybrid Heroes and Graphic Posthumanity: Comics as a Media Technology for Critical Posthumanism," which I discuss in more detail in chapter 4.
65. Coole and Frost, *New Materialisms*, 2.
66. Coole, *New Materialisms*, 9.
67. Coole, *New Materialisms*, 10.
68. Marx, *German Ideology*, 16.
69. Karasik and Newgarden, *How to Read "Nancy,"* 62.
70. Karasik and Newgarden, *How to Read "Nancy,"* 62–63.
71. Karasik and Newgarden, *How to Read "Nancy,"* 63.
72. Note that this conception of the ideal life for comic creation was shared by Bill Watterson, as I discuss above.
73. Jaimes, "Olivia Jaimes, the Mysterious Cartoonist," 125.
74. Jaimes, "Olivia Jaimes, the Mysterious Cartoonist," 125.
75. Kleefeld, *Webcomics*, 126.
76. Kleefeld, *Webcomics*, 200.
77. Morrison, *Playing in the Dark*, 16.
78. Guynes and Lund, "Not to Interpret," 11.
79. Haraway, "Situated Knowledges," 588.
80. Haraway, "Situated Knowledges," 590.
81. Haraway, *Staying with the Trouble*, 97.
82. Chute, *Why Comics?*, 240.
83. McCloud, *Reinventing Comics*, 200.
84. Kleefeld, *Webcomics*, 109.
85. Harris, *Kids These Days*, loc. 2261.

86. Jaimes, "Olivia Jaimes, the Mysterious Cartoonist," 126.
87. Read, "The Oatmeal Sucks."
88. Jaimes, "Olivia Jaimes, the Mysterious Cartoonist," 126.
89. Mead, "Scourge of Relatability."
90. Mead, "Scourge of Relatability."
91. Mead, "Scourge of Relatability."
92. Tompkins, "Introduction," xi, emphasis added.
93. Tompkins, "The Reader in History," 211.
94. Jiménez, "PoC, LGBTQ, and Gender," 439.
95. Nannicelli and Taberham, "Introduction," 4.
96. Boryczka and Disney, "Intersectionality for the Global Age," 447.
97. Crisp et al., "Complexities," 5.
98. Lavoie, "Why We Need Diverse Books."
99. Acevedo-Aquino et al., "Reflections," 28.
100. Rosenfield, "What Is #OwnVoices."
101. Smith, "Personal Connection."
102. Smith, "Personal Connection."
103. Smith, "Personal Connection."
104. Andrews McMeel Universal, "Andrews McMeel Syndication Announces."
105. Onion, "Awful Emptiness."
106. Onion, "Awful Emptiness."
107. Kanai, *Gender and Relatability*, 2. I will discuss the roles that race and class play in *Nancy* in chapter 2.
108. Kanai, *Gender and Relatability*, 2.
109. Kanai, *Gender and Relatability*, 3.
110. Kanai, *Gender and Relatability*, 32.
111. Jaimes, "Olivia Jaimes, the Mysterious Cartoonist," 125.
112. Groensteen, *System of Comics*, 254.
113. Groensteen, *System of Comics*, 207.
114. Groensteen, *System of Comics*, 210.
115. Postema, *Narrative Structure in Comics*, 120.
116. Postema, *Narrative Structure in Comics*, 120.
117. It should be noted that Postema's first example of how comics teach readers to read them is in fact a newspaper comic strip, Bill Watterson's *Calvin and Hobbes*: "What is striking about the *Calvin and Hobbes* example is that it is so mainstream. This is a newspaper strip going out to an audience that often reads the comics section incidentally, and may not read many other types of comics." Postema, *Narrative Structure in Comics*, 120.

118. Cavna, "For the First Time."

119. Price, "Walking in Nancy's Shoes," 131.

120. Gustines, "'Mark Trail' Jumps into an Adventure."

121. King Features Syndicate, "Flash Is Back!"

122. Abate, *Funny Girls*, 168.

123. Price, "Walking in Nancy's Shoes," 131.

124. Degg, "Karen Moy Is Worthy."

125. Howard, "Brief History," 41.

126. Howard, "Brief History," 41.

127. Howard, "Brief History," 41.

128. Howard, "Brief History," 43.

129. Wanzo, "It's a Hero?," 314.

1. "CASH PREFERRED"

1. Gordon, *Comic Strips and Consumer Culture*, 14.

2. Gordon, *Comic Strips and Consumer Culture*, 14.

3. Kanai, *Gender and Relatability*, 186.

4. Kanai, *Gender and Relatability*, 10.

5. Kelp-Stebbins, "Reading Spaces," 1.

6. Lefèvre, "Construction of Space," 159.

7. Lefèvre, "Construction of Space," 160.

8. Murray, "Scott Pilgrim," 130.

9. Murray, "Scott Pilgrim," 132.

10. Murray, "Scott Pilgrim," 133.

11. Kanai, *Gender and Relatability*, 184.

12. Harris, *Kids These Days*, loc. 1098.

13. Misemer, "Historical Approach to Webcomics," 16.

14. Misemer, "Historical Approach to Webcomics," 16.

15. Harris, *Kids These Days*, loc. 1056.

16. Kleefeld, *Webcomics*, 71.

17. Kleefeld, *Webcomics*, 71.

18. Misemer, "Historical Approach to Webcomics," 17.

19. McCloud, "Oh Crap," 269.

20. McCloud, "Oh Crap," 269.

21. McCloud, "Oh Crap," 270.

22. McCloud, "Oh Crap," 270, 271.

23. As I will discuss in chapter 2.

24. Kanai, *Gender and Relatability*, 9.

25. Kanai, *Gender and Relatability*, 11.

26. Kanai, *Gender and Relatability*, 11.

27. Cavna, "'Nancy' and Artist Olivia Jaimes."

28. I will discuss this strip in detail in both chapter 2 and chapter 3.

29. I will discuss this strip in more detail in chapter 3.

30. Walker, *Comics*, 194.

31. Scott, *Fake Geek Girls*, 208.

32. Scott, *Fake Geek Girls*, 208.

33. Carlin, "Nancy's Art Attack," 197–98.

34. Brainard, *Nancy Book*, 134–37.

35. Lauterbach, "Joe Brainard," 7.

36. Padgett, "Origins of Joe Brainard's Nancy," 27.

37. Padgett, "Origins of Joe Brainard's Nancy," 30.

38. Padgett, "Origins of Joe Brainard's Nancy," 30.

39. Lauterbach, "Joe Brainard," 8, 10, 11, 20.

40. Lauterbach, "Joe Brainard," 11.

41. Lauterbach, "Joe Brainard," 13.

42. Lauterbach, "Joe Brainard," 13.

43. Lauterbach, "Joe Brainard," 18.

44. Lauterbach, "Joe Brainard," 14.

45. In addition, Brainard produced sexually explicit works—such as *If Nancy Was an Underground Comic Character*, *If Nancy Made Blue Movies*, *If Nancy Was a Sailor's Basket*, and *If Nancy Was a Boy*—which, according to Lauterbach, "expose and alleviate our anxiety [and] play havoc with propriety [as] Joe/Nancy neutralizes and naturalizes codes of gender identification, subtly shifting the expected frame to complicate our gaze." Lauterbach, "Joe Brainard," 21.

46. Lauterbach, "Joe Brainard," 23.

47. Cavna, "Is It Time."

48. *Des Moines Register*, August 14, 2019.

49. Hatfield, *Alternative Comics*, 2–3.

50. Tawa, "Beloved 'Peanuts' Creator."

51. Boom! Entertainment, "Peanuts."

52. Schulz and Melendez, *Peanuts*, back cover.

53. Karasik and Newgarden, *How to Read "Nancy,"* 65.

54. Gordon, *Comic Strips and Consumer Culture*, 31.

55. Gordon, *Comic Strips and Consumer Culture*, 32.

56. Gordon, *Comic Strips and Consumer Culture*, 33.

57. Gordon, *Comic Strips and Consumer Culture*, 47.

58. I discuss the online commentary about Jaimes's *Nancy* in chapter 2, including the condemnation of her work by many fans of Bushmiller.

59. Booth, *Playing Fans*, 1.

60. Booth, *Playing Fans*, 7.
61. Booth, *Playing Fans*, 7.
62. Booth, *Playing Fans*, 1.
63. Rivera, "Dudes be sliding into my DMs."
64. Jaimes, "Olivia Jaimes, the Mysterious Cartoonist," 124.
65. Andrews McMeel Universal, "Andrews McMeel Syndication Announces."

2. "NEW YEAR, NEW ME!"

1. Fritzi speaks from outside the panel on April 25 when we see her speech bubble yelling at Nancy. Fritzi also briefly appears in the strip on May 14, 15, and 25, but she does not speak.
2. Kukonnen, *Studying Comics*, 16.
3. See my discussion of this strip in chapter 1.
4. Jaimes, "Olivia Jaimes, the Mysterious Cartoonist," 128.
5. Jaimes, "Olivia Jaimes, the Mysterious Cartoonist," 128.
6. Scott, *Fake Geek Girls*, 7.
7. McCloud, "Five Card Nancy."
8. Chute, *Why Comics?*, 11.
9. Qtd. in Chute, *Why Comics?*, 219.
10. Karasik and Newgarden, *How to Read "Nancy,"* 24.
11. Griffith, introduction, n.p.
12. Griffith, *Are We Having Fun Yet?*, 51.
13. Griffith, *Are We Having Fun Yet?*, 61.
14. Griffith, *Are We Having Fun Yet?*, 51–53.
15. Griffith, introduction, n.p.
16. Brunetti, introduction, n.p.
17. Shaw, "Grown Men Reading 'Nancy.'"
18. The April 30 strip, which I've discussed in more detail in the previous chapter, would have been written well in advance of the April 24 comment, as daily comic strips are usually written months before they see publication, as I discuss in chapter 4 of this book.
19. Karasik and Newgarden, *How to Read "Nancy,"* 47.
20. Karasik and Newgarden, *How to Read "Nancy,"* 52.
21. Kennedy, "Statuesque of Liberty."
22. Heintjes, "Fritzi Ritz before Bushmiller."
23. Heintjes, "Fritzi Ritz before Bushmiller."
24. Rivera, "Side note."
25. Andersen, "*Sarah's Scribbles.*"
26. Kleefeld, *Webcomics*, 80.

27. Kleefeld, *Webcomics*, 81.

28. Coole and Frost, *New Materialisms*, 10.

29. Jaimes, "Olivia Jaimes, the Mysterious Cartoonist," 127.

30. Kelp-Stebbins, "Reading Spaces," 3.

31. Kelp-Stebbins, "Reading Spaces," 3.

32. Kelp-Stebbins, "Reading Spaces," 4.

33. Abate, *Funny Girls*, 1.

34. Abate, *Funny Girls*, 6, 8.

35. Abate, *Funny Girls*, 16.

36. Jaimes, "Olivia Jaimes, the Mysterious Cartoonist," 126.

37. Jaimes, "Olivia Jaimes, the Mysterious Cartoonist," 126.

38. Jaimes, "Olivia Jaimes, the Mysterious Cartoonist," 126.

39. Johnston, "Have a Question?"

40. Jaimes, "Olivia Jaimes, the Mysterious Cartoonist," 129.

41. Kanai, *Gender and Relatability*, 53.

42. Kanai, *Gender and Relatability*, 55–56.

43. Kanai, *Gender and Relatability*, 56.

44. Kanai, *Gender and Relatability*, 54.

45. Kanai, *Gender and Relatability*, 54.

46. Abate, *Funny Girls*, 13.

47. Abate, *Funny Girls*, 13.

48. Wanzo, *Content of Our Caricature*, 5.

49. C. Johnson, foreword, 7.

50. White and Fuentez, "Analysis of Black Images," 72.

51. Nama, *Super Black*, 6.

52. Kamp, "Guess Who's Coming to 'Peanuts,'" 1.

53. Isaacs, "Charles Schultz," 97.

54. Wanzo, *Content of Our Caricature*, 4.

55. Kamp, "Guess Who's Coming to 'Peanuts,'" 2.

56. Lei and Delahoussaye, "'Peanuts' First Black Character Franklin."

57. Lei and Delahoussaye, "'Peanuts' First Black Character Franklin."

58. Lei and Delahoussaye, "'Peanuts' First Black Character Franklin."

59. Karasik and Newgarden, *How to Read "Nancy,"* 86.

60. Abate, *Funny Girls*, 9.

61. Abate, *Funny Girls*, 9.

62. Abate, *Funny Girls*, 56.

63. Sammond, *Birth of an Industry*, 3.

64. Sammond, *Birth of an Industry*, 133.

65. Abate, *Funny Girls*, 59.

66. Meskin, "Defining Comics?," 374.

67. Gateward and Jennings, "Introduction," 3.
68. Gateward and Jennings, "Introduction," 3.
69. Gateward and Jennings, "Introduction," 3.
70. Gateward and Jennings, "Introduction," 3.
71. Carrier, "Relevant."
72. Francis, "American Truths," 137.
73. Wanzo, *Content of Our Caricature*, 115.
74. Francis, "American Truths," 138.
75. Francis, "American Truths," 140.
76. Francis, "American Truths," 141.
77. Burke, *Colorblind Racism*, 1–2.
78. Burke, *Colorblind Racism*, 3–4.
79. Burke, *Colorblind Racism*, 78.
80. White and Fuentez, "Analysis of Black Images," 72.
81. Cyree, "Contemporary Representations," 100.
82. Cyree, "Contemporary Representations," 109.
83. White and Fuentez, "Analysis of Black Images," 75.
84. Berlatsky and Dagbovie-Mullins, "Whiteness of the Whale," 47.
85. I will discuss the robotics club in more detail in chapter 3.
86. Berlatsky and Dagbovie-Mullins, "Whiteness of the Whale," 47–48.
87. Berlatsky and Dagbovie-Mullins, "Whiteness of the Whale," 48.
88. Berlatsky and Dagbovie-Mullins, "Whiteness of the Whale," 54.
89. Berlatsky and Dagbovie-Mullins, "Whiteness of the Whale," 54.
90. Henderson, "Representation Matters."
91. Henderson, "Representation Matters."
92. Jiménez, "PoC, LGBTQ, and Gender," 435.
93. Jiménez, "PoC, LGBTQ, and Gender," 435, 440, 443.
94. See my discussion of #OwnVoices in my introduction.
95. Jiménez, "PoC, LGBTQ, and Gender," 442.
96. Brooks, "Reading Representations of Themselves," 373.
97. Brooks, "Reading Representations of Themselves," 373.
98. Brooks, "Reading Representations of Themselves," 380.
99. Brooks, "Reading Representations of Themselves," 390.

3. "BUT I BROKE THE FOURTH WALL!"
1. Roberts, "Novelty Cookie Jar."
2. Lefèvre, "Construction of Space," 157.
3. Inge, "Form and Function," 2.
4. Inge, "Form and Function," 3.
5. Inge, "Form and Function," 6.

6. Inge, "Form and Function," 7.

7. Inge, "Form and Function," 9.

8. Szép, *Comics and the Body*, 82.

9. Szép, *Comics and the Body*, 82.

10. Szép, *Comics and the Body*, 83.

11. Szép, *Comics and the Body*, 86.

12. Szép, *Comics and the Body*, 93.

13. Szép, *Comics and the Body*, 46.

14. Szép, *Comics and the Body*, 46–47.

15. Snapchat filters were invented in 2015. Called "lenses" at the time, they allowed users to add effects to selfies. As one article puts it, "Rainbow barf [was] an instant hit," and Snapchat's popularity grew so that it had over 100 million "daily active users" by the end of 2015. See Bell, "Briefing on the History." The humor of this strip depends on a reader knowing what a Snapchat filter is and why it might make Nancy and Sluggo look different.

16. Hague, *Comics and the Senses*, 25.

17. Kashtan, *Between Pen and Pixel*, 69.

18. Kashtan, *Between Pen and Pixel*, 69.

19. Jenkins, *Comics and Stuff*, 3.

20. Jenkins, *Comics and Stuff*, 17.

21. Dinnen, "Things That Matter," 314.

22. Dinnen, "Things That Matter," 315.

23. Dinnen, "Things That Matter," 327.

24. Dinnen, "Things That Matter," 320.

25. Harman, *Guerilla Metaphysics*, 9.

26. Harman, *Guerilla Metaphysics*, 94.

27. Harman, *Guerilla Metaphysics*, 101.

28. Harman, *Guerilla Metaphysics*, 130.

29. Harman, *Guerilla Metaphysics*, 131.

30. Coole and Frost, *New Materialisms*, 7.

31. Hague, *Comics and the Senses*, 5.

32. Kelp-Stebbins, "Hybrid Heroes," 331.

33. Kelp-Stebbins, "Hybrid Heroes," 332.

34. Kelp-Stebbins, "Hybrid Heroes," 331.

35. Kelp-Stebbins, "Hybrid Heroes," 345.

36. Kelp-Stebbins, "Hybrid Heroes," 340.

37. Kelp-Stebbins, "Hybrid Heroes," 336.

38. Kelp-Stebbins, "Hybrid Heroes," 335.

39. Kelp-Stebbins, "Hybrid Heroes," 335.

40. Kelp-Stebbins, "Hybrid Heroes," 335.
41. Kelp-Stebbins, "Hybrid Heroes," 335.
42. Harman, *Guerilla Metaphysics*, 105.
43. Harman, *Guerilla Metaphysics*, 105.
44. Morton, *Hyperobjects*, 23.
45. Morton, *Hyperobjects*, 112.
46. Morton, *Hyperobjects*, 124.
47. Kelp-Stebbins, "Hybrid Heroes," 337.
48. Know Your Memes, "Sluggo Is Lit," under "Images."
49. Jaimes, "Olivia Jaimes, the Mysterious Cartoonist," 128.
50. Kelp-Stebbins, "Reading Spaces," 1.
51. Kelp-Stebbins, "Reading Spaces," 2.
52. Kelp-Stebbins, "Hybrid Heroes," 337.
53. Kelp-Stebbins, "Hybrid Heroes," 340.
54. McCloud, *Understanding Comics*, 206.
55. Karasik and Newgarden, *How to Read "Nancy,"* 137.

4. "YOU'VE GOT YOUR MASK, RIGHT?"

1. Edwards, "Pandemic Gives the Funny Pages a Jolt," 1.
2. Edwards, "Pandemic Gives the Funny Pages a Jolt," 4.
3. Edwards, "Pandemic Gives the Funny Pages a Jolt," 4.
4. Fruhlinger, "Should the Funny Pages," 2.
5. Fruhlinger, "Should the Funny Pages," 2.
6. Fruhlinger, "Should the Funny Pages," 9.
7. Fruhlinger, "Should the Funny Pages," 8.
8. Fruhlinger, "Should the Funny Pages," 8.
9. Jarvis, "Censorship on the Comics Page," 3.
10. Jarvis, "Censorship on the Comics Page," 4.
11. Jarvis, "Censorship on the Comics Page," 9.
12. Heintjes, "Big Deals."
13. Trudeau, "Death and Politics," 87.
14. Sills, "Inappropriate Political Content," 353–54.
15. Richardson, "Gannett."
16. I realize that drawing a strict line between the "social" and the "political" is not fully possible. For my purposes, "political" refers to direct mentions of specific governmental policies.
17. Saji, Venkatesan, and Callender, "Comics in the Time of a Pan(dem)ic," 142.
18. Callender et al., "Art of Medicine," 1063.
19. Callender et al., "Art of Medicine," 1062.

20. Callender et al., "Art of Medicine," 1062.
21. Jaimes, "Olivia Jaimes, the Mysterious Cartoonist," 129.
22. Moore, "E(a)ffective Precarity," 125.
23. Moore, "E(a)ffective Precarity," 126, 130.
24. Moore, "E(a)ffective Precarity," 132.
25. Caplan-Bricker, "Is Online Test-Monitoring Here to Stay?"
26. Caplan-Bricker, "Is Online Test-Monitoring Here to Stay?"
27. Caplan-Bricker, "Is Online Test-Monitoring Here to Stay?"
28. Spearman, "Student's TikTok."
29. Many more examples of how college students have been affected by proctoring software can be found on Twitter accounts such as @Procteario and @ProcterrorU. Caplan-Bricker, "Is Online Test-Monitoring Here to Stay?"
30. Caplan-Bricker, "Is Online Test-Monitoring Here to Stay?"
31. Caplan-Bricker, "Is Online Test-Monitoring Here to Stay?"
32. García-Bullé, "Surveillance in Proctored Exams."
33. Caplan-Bricker, "Is Online Test-Monitoring Here to Stay?"
34. Caplan-Bricker, "Is Online Test-Monitoring Here to Stay?"
35. Geiger, "Students Are Easily Cheating."
36. Geiger, "Students Are Easily Cheating."

BIBLIOGRAPHY

Abate, Michelle Ann. *Funny Girls: Guffaws, Guts, and Gender in Classic American Comics*. Jackson: University Press of Mississippi, 2019.

Acevedo-Aquino, Maria V., David Bowles, Jill Eisenberg, Zetta Elliott, Jesse Gainer, and Nancy Valdez-Gainer. "Reflections on the #OwnVoices Movement." *Journal of Children's Literature* 46, no. 2 (2020): 27–35.

Andersen, Sarah. "*Sarah's Scribbles*: Interview with Sarah Andersen." By Cale. *Things in Squares* (blog), October 22, 2015. https://www .thingsinsquares.com/blog/sarahs-scribbles-interviews-with -webcomic-artists/.

Andrews McMeel Universal. "Andrews McMeel Syndication Announces Olivia Jaimes as Newest 'Nancy' Cartoonist." Andrews McMeel Syndication, press release, April 6, 2018. http://syndication .andrewsmcmeel.com/press/press_release/217.

Bartosch, Simon. "Understanding Comics' Mediality as an Actor-Network: Some Elements of Translation in the Works of Brian Fies and Dylan Horrocks." *Journal of Graphic Novels and Comics* 7, no. 3 (2016): 242–53.

Beaty, Bart. *Comics versus Art*. Toronto: University of Toronto Press, 2012.

Bell, Karissa. "A Briefing on the History of Snapchat Updates." Mashable, February 4, 2017. https://mashable.com/article/snapchat-updates-five-year.

Berlatsky, Eric, and Sika Dagbovie-Mullins. "The Whiteness of the Whale and the Darkness of the Dinosaur: The Africanist Presence in Superhero Comics from *Black Lightning* to *Moon Girl*." In *Unstable Masks: Whiteness and American Superhero Comics*, edited by Sean Guynes and Martin Lund, 38–56. Columbus: The Ohio State University Press, 2020.

Boom! Entertainment. "Peanuts." Boom! Studios. Accessed January 12, 2023. https://web.archive.org/web/20210924184314/https://shop .boom-studios.com/collections/peanuts.

Booth, Paul. *Playing Fans: Negotiating Fandom and Media in the Digital Age*. Iowa City: University of Iowa Press, 2015.

Boryczka, Jocelyn M., and Jennifer Leigh Disney. "Intersectionality for the Global Age." *New Political Science* 37, no. 4 (2015): 447–57.

Brainard, Joe. *The Nancy Book*. Edited by Lisa Pearson and Ron Padgett. Los Angeles: Siglio Press, 2008.

Brooks, Wanda. "Reading Representations of Themselves: Urban Youth Use Culture and African American Textual Features to Develop Literary Understandings." *Reading Research Quarterly* 41, no. 3 (July–September 2006): 372–92.

Brown, Megan. "Survival at Work: Flexibility and Adaptability in American Corporate Culture." *Cultural Studies* 17, no. 5 (2003): 713–33.

Brunetti, Ivan. Introduction to *Nancy Loves Sluggo*, edited by Eric Reynold. Seattle: Fantagraphics Books, 2014.

Burke, Meghan. *Colorblind Racism*. New York: Polity Press, 2019.

Callender, Brian, Shirlene Obuobi, M. K. Czerwiec, and Ian Williams. "The Art of Medicine: COVID-19, Comics, and the Visual Culture of Contagion." *Lancet*, October 2020, 1061–63.

Caplan-Bricker, Nora. "Is Online Test-Monitoring Here to Stay?" *New Yorker*, May 27, 2021. https://www.newyorker.com/tech/annals-of -technology/is-online-test-monitoring-here-to-stay.

Carlin, John. "Nancy's Art Attack." In *The Best of Ernie Bushmiller's "Nancy,"* edited by Brian Walker, 196–99. Wilton CT: Comicana Books, 1988.

Carrier, James. "Relevant Comics . . . Cartoonists Break Old Taboos; Some Don't Change." *Mansfield News Journal*, January 7, 1973, 58.

Cavna, Michael. "For the First Time in Her 85 Years, 'Nancy' Will Be Drawn by a Woman." *Washington Post*, April 18, 2018. https://www .washingtonpost.com/news/comic-riffs/wp/2018/04/08/for-the-first -time-in-her-85-years-nancy-will-be-drawn-by-a-woman/.

———. "Is It Time to Bottle 'Blondie'? Now's Your Chance to Defend That 'Toon." *Comic Riffs* (blog), August 14, 2019. http://voices.washingtonpost .com/comic-riffs/2009/09/blondie_defend_that_toon.html.

———. "'Nancy' and Artist Olivia Jaimes Continue to Make the Comics Page 'Lit' One Year In." *Washington Post*, April 9, 2019. https://www .washingtonpost.com/arts-entertainment/2019/04/09/nancy-artist -olivia-jaimes-continue-make-comics-page-lit-one-year/.

Chute, Hillary. *Why Comics? From Underground to Everywhere*. New York: Harper Collins, 2017.

Coole, Diana, and Samantha Frost, eds. *New Materialisms: Ontology, Agency, and Politics*. Durham NC: Duke University Press, 2010.

Crisp, Thomas, Mary Napoli, Vivian Yenika-Agbaw, and Angie Zapata. "The Complexities of #OwnVoices in Children's Literature." *Journal of Children's Literature* 46, no. 2 (2020): 5–7.

Cyree, Tia T. M. "Contemporary Representations of Black Females in Newspaper Comic Strips." In *Black Comics: Politics of Race and Representation*, edited by Sheena C. Howard and Ronald L. Jackson II, 88–121. New York: Bloomsbury Press, 2015.

Degg, D. D. "Karen Moy Is Worthy." Daily Cartoonist, August 30, 2018. https://www.dailycartoonist.com/index.php/2018/08/30/karen-moy-is-worthy/.

Dinnen, Zara. "Things That Matter: Representing Everyday Technological Things in Comics." *Studies in Comics* 3, no. 2 (2012): 313–29.

Edwards, Gavin. "A Pandemic Gives the Funny Pages a Jolt of Reality." *New York Times*, April 27, 2020. https://www.nytimes.com/2020/04/27/arts/design/comic-strips-coronavirus.html.

Flaherty, Colleen. "Big Proctor: Is the Fight against Cheating during Remote Instruction Worth Enlisting Third-Party Student Surveillance Platforms?" Inside Higher Ed, May 11, 2020. https://www.insidehighered.com/news/2020/05/11/online-proctoring-surging-during-covid-19.

Francis, Consuela. "American Truths: Blackness and the American Superhero." In *The Blacker the Ink: Constructions of Black Identity in Comics and Sequential Art*, edited by Frances Gateward and John Jennings, 137–52. New Brunswick NJ: Rutgers University Press, 2015.

Fruhlinger, Josh. "Should the Funny Pages Look like the News?" Polygon, June 10, 2020. https://www.polygon.com/comics/2020/6/10/21284457/coronavirus-comic-strips-funny-pages-newspapers.

García-Bullé, Sofía. "Surveillance in Proctored Exams: How Much Is Too Much?" Translation by Daniel Wetta. Institute for the Future of Education, November 2, 2020. https://observatory.tec.mx/edu-news/proctored-surveillance.

Gateward, Frances, and John Jennings. "Introduction: The Sweeter the Christmas." In *The Blacker the Ink: Constructions of Black Identity in Comics and Sequential Art*, edited by Frances Gateward and John Jennings, 1–18. New Brunswick NJ: Rutgers University Press, 2015.

Geiger, Gabriel. "Students Are Easily Cheating 'State-of-the-Art' Test Proctoring Tech." Vice, March 5, 2021. https://www.vice.com/en/article/3an98j/students-are-easily-cheating-state-of-the-art-test-proctoring-tech.

Goldstein, Nancy. "Fashion in the Funny Papers: Cartoonist Jackie Ormes's American Look." In *The Blacker the Ink: Constructions of Black Identity in Comics and Sequential Art*, edited by Frances Gateward and John Jennings, 95–116. New Brunswick NJ: Rutgers University Press, 2015.

———. "The Trouble with Romance in Jackie Ormes's Comics." In *Black Comics: Politics of Race and Representation*, edited by Sheena C. Howard and Ronald L. Jackson II, 51–87. New York: Bloomsbury Press, 2015.

Gordon, Ian. *Comic Strips and Consumer Culture, 1890–1945*. Washington DC: Smithsonian Institution Press, 1998.

Grieco, Elizabeth. "Fast Facts about the Newspaper Industry's Financial Struggles as McClatchy Files for Bankruptcy." Pew Research Center, February 14, 2020. https://www.pewresearch.org/fact-tank/2020/02/14/fast-facts-about-the-newspaper-industrys-financial-struggles.

Griffith, Bill. *Are We Having Fun Yet? Zippy the Pinhead's 29 Day Guide to Random Activities and Arbitrary Donuts*. Seattle: Fantagraphics Books, 1985.

———. Introduction to *Nancy Likes Christmas*, edited by Kim Thompson. Seattle: Fantagraphics Books, 2012.

Groensteen, Thierry. *The System of Comics*. Translated by Bart Beaty and Nick Nguyen. Jackson: University Press of Mississippi, 2007.

Gustines, George Gene. "'Mark Trail' Jumps into an Adventure with a New Cartoonist." *New York Times*, September 25, 2020. https://www.nytimes.com/2020/09/25/arts/mark-trail-new-cartoonist.html.

Guynes, Sean, and Martin Lund. "Not to Interpret, but to Abolish: Whiteness Studies and American Superhero Comics." In *Unstable Masks: Whiteness and American Superhero Comics*, edited by Sean Guynes and Martin Lund, 1–16. Columbus: The Ohio State University Press, 2020.

Hague, Ian. *Comics and the Senses: A Multisensory Approach to Comics and Graphic Novels*. London: Routledge Press, 2014.

Haraway, Donna. "Situated Knowledges: The Science Question in Feminism and the Privilege of Partial Perspective." *Feminist Studies* 14, no. 3 (1988): 575–99.

———. *Staying with the Trouble: Making Kin in the Chthulucene*. Durham NC: Duke University Press, 2016.

Harman, Graham. *Guerilla Metaphysics: Phenomenology and the Carpentry of Things*. Chicago: Carus Publishing, 2005.

——— . *Object-Oriented Ontology: A New Theory of Everything*. London: Pelican Books, 2007.

Harris, Malcolm. *Kids These Days: Human Capital and the Making of Millennials*. New York: Little, Brown, and Company, 2017. Kindle.

Hatfield, Charles. *Alternative Comics: An Emerging Literature*. Jackson: University of Mississippi Press, 2005.

Heer, Jeet. Afterword to *Black Comics: Politics of Race and Representation*, edited by Sheena C. Howard and Ronald L. Jackson II, 423–32. New York: Bloomsbury Press, 2015.

Heintjes, Tom. "Big Deals: Comics' Highest Profile Moments." *Hogan's Alley* 7 (1999). https://web.archive.org/web/20130630083743/http:/cartoonician.com/big-deals-comics-highest-profile-moments/.

——— . "Fritzi Ritz before Bushmiller: She's Come a Long Way, Baby!" *Hogan's Alley* 7 (1999). https://www.hoganmag.com/blog/fritzi-ritz-before-bushmiller-shes-come-a-long-way-baby.

Henderson, Mary J. "Representation Matters: Post-Racial Tensions in *Moon Girl* and *Devil Dinosaur*." *ImageText* 10, no. 3 (2019). https://imagetextjournal.com/representation-matters-post-racial-tensions-in-moon-girl-and-devil-dinosaur/.

Howard, Sheena C. "Brief History of the Black Comic Strip: Past and Present." In *Black Comics: Politics of Race and Representation*, edited by Sheena C. Howard and Ronald L. Jackson II, 31–50. New York: Bloomsbury Press, 2015.

Howard, Sheena C., and Ronald L. Jackson II. Introduction to *Black Comics: Politics of Race and Representation*, edited by Sheena C. Howard and Ronald L. Jackson II, 17–30. New York: Bloomsbury Press, 2015.

Inge, M. Thomas. "Form and Function in Metacomics: Self-Reflexivity in the Comic Strips." *Studies in Popular Culture* 13, no. 2 (1991): 1–10.

Isaacs, Stan. "Charles Schulz: 'Comic Strips Aren't Art.'" In *Charles M. Schulz: Conversations*, edited by Thomas Inge, 86–97. Jackson: University Press of Mississippi, 2020.

Jaimes, Olivia. "Olivia Jaimes, the Mysterious Cartoonist behind *Nancy*, Gives Rare Interview." Interview by Abraham Reisman, in *Nancy: A Comic Collection*, by Olivia Jaimes. Kansas City MO: Andrews McMeel Publishing, 2019.

Jarvis, Eric. "Censorship on the Comics Page: Walt Kelly's 'Pogo' and American Political Culture in the Cold War Era." *Studies in Popular Culture* 26, no. 1 (2003): 1–13.

Jenkins, Henry. *Comics and Stuff*. New York: NYU Press, 2020.

Jerome, Rocko. "I Have Seen Olivia Jaimes, the Cartoonist behind the New *Nancy*." Rocko Jerome's official website, October 1, 2018. https://rockojerome.com/2018/10/01/i-have-seen-olivia-jaimes-the -cartoonist-behind-the-new-nancy/.

Jiménez, Laura M. "PoC, LGBTQ, and Gender: The Intersectionality of America Chavez." *Journal of Lesbian Studies* 22, no. 4 (2018): 435–45.

Johnson, Charles. Foreword to *Black Images in the Comics: A Visual History*, edited by Fredrik Strömberg, 5–19. Seattle: Fantagraphics Books, 2003.

Johnson, Derek. "Fantagonism, Franchising, and Industry Management of Fan Privilege." In *The Routledge Companion to Media Fandom*, edited by Melissa A. Click and Suzanne Scott, 395–405. London: Routledge Press, 2018.

Johnston, Lynne. "Have a Question?" *For Better or For Worse* official website. Accessed November 2, 2020. https://www.fborfw.com/behind _the_scenes/faq/.

Kamp, David. "Guess Who's Coming to 'Peanuts.'" *New York Times*, January 13, 2018. https://www.nytimes.com/2018/01/13/opinion/sunday /peanuts-franklin-charlie-brown.html.

Kanai, Akane. *Gender and Relatability in Digital Culture: Managing Affect, Intimacy and Value*. New York: Palgrave Macmillan, 2019.

Karasik, Paul, and Mark Newgarden. *How to Read "Nancy": The Elements of Comics in Three Easy Panels*. Seattle: Fantagraphics Books, 2017.

Kashtan, Aaron. *Between Pen and Pixel: Comics, Materiality, and the Book of the Future*. Columbus: The Ohio State University Press, 2018.

Kelp-Stebbins, Katherine. "Hybrid Heroes and Graphic Posthumanity: Comics as a Media Technology for Critical Posthumanism." *Studies in Comics* 3, no. 2 (2012): 331–48.

———. "Reading Spaces: The Politics of Page Layout." In *The Oxford Handbook of Comic Book Studies*, edited by Frederick Luis Aldama, 1–20. Oxford University Press, 2018.

Kennedy, Bob. "The Statuesque of Liberty." *Hogan's Alley* 8 (2000). https:// www.hoganmag.com/blog/the-statuesque-of-liberty.

King Features Syndicate. "Flash Is Back! King Features Celebrates the 40th Anniversary of the Original *Flash Gordon* Film." *King Features* (blog), November 16, 2020. https://kingfeatures.com/2020/11/flash-is -back-king-features-celebrates-the40th-anniversary-of-the-original -flash-gordon-film/.

Kleefeld, Sean. *Webcomics*. Bloomsbury Comics Studies. New York: Bloomsbury Press, 2020.

Know Your Meme. S.v. "Sluggo Is Lit." By Matt. Accessed May 4, 2021.
    https://knowyourmeme.com/memes/sluggo-is-lit/photos.

Kukkonen, Karin. *Studying Comics and Graphic Novels*. New York: Wiley,
    2013.

Lauterbach, Ann. "Joe Brainard and Nancy." In *The Nancy Book*, edited by
    Lisa Pearson and Ron Padgett, 7–26. Los Angeles: Siglio Press, 2008.

Lavoie, Alaina. "Why We Need Diverse Books Is No Longer Using the
    Term #OwnVoices." We Need Diverse Books, press release, June 6,
    2021. https://diversebooks.org/why-we-need-diverse-books-is-no
    -longer-using-the-term-ownvoices/.

Lefèvre, Pascal. "The Construction of Space in Comics." In *A Comics
    Study Reader*, edited by Jeet Heer and Kent Worcester, 157–62. Jack-
    son: University of Mississippi Press, 2009.

Lei, Cecelia, and James Delahoussaye. "'Peanuts' First Black Character
    Franklin Turns 50." *Weekend Edition Sunday*, July 29, 2018. https://
    www.npr.org/2018/07/29/633544308/peanuts-character-franklin
    -turns-50.

Lorey, Isabell. *State of Insecurity: Government of the Precarious*. Translated
    by Aileen Derieg. New York: Verso, 2015.

Marx, Karl, and Frederick Engels. *The German Ideology Part One, with
    Selections from Parts Two and Three, Together with Marx's "Introduc-
    tion to a Critique of Political Economy."* New York: International
    Publishers, 2001.

McCloud, Scott. "Five Card Nancy." Scott McCloud's official website.
    Accessed April 12, 2021. http://www.scottmccloud.com/4-inventions
    /nancy/.

———. "Oh Crap—Webcomics!" In *The Best American Comics, 2014*,
    edited by Scott McCloud and Bill Kartalopoulos, 269–72. New York:
    Houghton, Mifflin, Harcourt, 2014.

———. *Reinventing Comics: The Evolution of an Art Form*. New York:
    Perennial Press, 2000.

———. *Understanding Comics: The Invisible Art*. New York: Harper Col-
    lins, 1993.

Mead, Rebecca. "The Scourge of Relatability." *New Yorker*, August 1, 2014.
    https://www.newyorker.com/culture/cultural-comment/scourge
    -relatability.

Meskin, Aaron. "Defining Comics?" *Journal of Aesthetics and Art Criticism*
    65, no. 4 (Autumn 2007): 369–79.

Misemer, Leah. "A Historical Approach to Webcomics: Digital Authorship
    in the Early 2000s." *Comics Grid* 9, no. 1 (2019): 1–21.

Moeller, Robin A., and Kim Becnel. "Drawing Diversity: Representations of Race in Graphic Novels for Young Adults." *School Library Research* 21 (2018). https://files.eric.ed.gov/fulltext/EJ1182162.pdf.

Moore, Phoebe V. "E(a)ffective Precarity, Control and Resistance in the Digitalised Workplace." In *Digital Objects, Digital Subjects: Interdisciplinary Perspectives on Capitalism, Labour and Politics in the Age of Big Data*, edited by David Chandler and Christian Fuchs. London: University of Westminster Press, 2019.

Morrison, Toni. *Playing in the Dark: Whiteness and the Literary Imagination*. New York: Vintage Press, 1993.

Morton, Timothy. *Hyperobjects: Philosophy and Ecology after the End of the World*. Minneapolis: University of Minnesota Press, 2013.

Murray, Padmini Ray. "Scott Pilgrim vs the Future of Comics Publishing." *Studies in Comics* 3, no. 1 (2012): 129–42.

Nama, Adilifu. *Super Black: American Pop Culture and Black Superheroes*. Austin: University of Texas Press, 2011.

Nannicelli, Ted, and Paul Taberham. "Introduction: Contemporary Cognitive Media Theory." In *Cognitive Media Theory*, edited by Ted Nannicelli and Paul Taberham, 1–23. New York: Routledge Press, 2014.

Onion, Rebecca. "The Awful Emptiness of 'Relatable.'" Slate, April 11, 2014. https://slate.com/human-interest/2014/04/relatable-the-adjective-is-everywhere-in-high-scchool-and-college-discussions-of-fiction-film-and-other-popular-culture-but-it-doesn-t-mean-anything.html.

Padgett, Ron. "The Origins of Joe Brainard's Nancy." In *The Nancy Book*, edited by Lisa Pearson and Ron Padgett, 27–30. Los Angeles: Siglio Press, 2008.

Postema, Barbara. *Narrative Structure in Comics: Making Sense of Fragments*. Rochester NY: RIT Press, 2013.

Price, Hilary B. "Walking in Nancy's Shoes: The Long Mile for Ernie Bushmiller to Olivia Jaimes." In *Nancy: A Comic Collection*, by Olivia Jaimes, 131–34. Kansas City MO: Andrews McMeel Publishing, 2019.

Priego, Ernesto. "On Cultural Materialism, Comics and Digital Media." *Opticon 1826*, no. 9 (Autumn 2020): 1–3. http://dx.doi.org/10.5334/opt.091007.

Read, Max. "The Oatmeal Sucks, Even If Buzzfeed Was Wrong." *Gawker*, December 17, 2012. https://www.gawker.com/5968009/the-oatmeal-sucks-even-if-buzzfeed-was-wrong.

Richardson, Valerie. "Gannett: 'Mallard Fillmore' Comic 'Did Not Meet Our Standards.'" *Washington Times*, March 4, 2021. https://www.washingtontimes.com/news/2021/mar/4/gannett-mallard-fillmore-comic-did-not-meet-our-st/

Rivera, Jules (@julesrivera). "Dudes be sliding into my DMs begging me to give it up." Twitter, November 18, 2020. https://twitter.com/julesrivera/status/1329274500685336576.

———. "Side note: nobody stopped from scripting about teenage girls shipping Mark with a peacock and here we are. Pea/Mark." Twitter, November 19, 2020. https://twitter.com/julesrivera/status/1329449050433867783.

Roberts, Kathleen. "Novelty Cookie Jar." LoveToKnow. Accessed July 12, 2020. https://antiques.lovetoknow.com/Novelty_Cookie_Jar.

Rosenfield, Kat. "What Is #OwnVoices Doing to Our Books?" Refinery 29, April 9, 2019. https://www.refinery29.com/en-us/2019/04/228847/own-voices-movement-ya-literature-impact.

Ross, Andrew. Nice Work If You Can Get It: Life and Labor in Precarious Times. New York: NYU Press, 2009.

Saji, Sweetha, Sathyaraj Venkatesan, and Brian Callender. "Comics in the Time of a Pan(dem)ic: COVID-19, Graphic Medicine, and Metaphors." Perspectives in Biology and Medicine 64, no. 1 (Winter 2021): 136–54.

Sammond, Nicholas. Birth of an Industry: Blackface Minstrelsy and the Rise of American Animation. Durham NC: Duke University Press, 2015.

Schulz, Charles M., and Bill Melendez. Peanuts: Scotland Bound, Charlie Brown. Adapted by Jason Cooper. Art by Robert Pope. Los Angeles: KaBoom! Press, 2021.

Scott, Suzanne. Fake Geek Girls: Fandom, Gender, and the Convergence Culture Industry. New York: NYU Press, 2019.

Shaw, Dash. "Grown Men Reading 'Nancy.'" New York Review of Books Daily, March 17, 2018. https://www.nybooks.com/daily/2018/03/17/grown-men-reading-nancy/?printpage=true.

Sills, Elizabeth. "Inappropriate Political Content: Serialized Comic Strips at the Intersection of Visual Rhetoric and the Rhetoric of Humor." In Black Comics: Politics of Race and Representation, edited by Sheena C. Howard and Ronald L. Jackson II, 351–76. New York: Bloomsbury Press, 2015.

Smith, S. E. "Personal Connection: #OwnVoices, Outing, and the Ongoing Quest for Authenticity." Bitch Media, October 14, 2020. https://www.bitchmedia.org/article/own-voices-outing-authors-credibility.

Spearman, Kahron. "Student's TikTok Shows Just How Harmful ProctorU Can Be." Daily Dot, October 2, 2020. https://www.dailydot.com/debug/student-proctoru-harmful-tiktok-video/.

Szép, Eszter. Comics and the Body: Drawing, Reading, and Vulnerability. Columbus: The Ohio State University Press, 2020.

Tawa, Renee. "Beloved 'Peanuts' Creator Is Mourned Worldwide." *Los Angeles Times*, February 14, 2000. https://www.latimes.com/archives /la-xpm-2000-feb-14-mn-64288-story.html.

Tompkins, Jane P. "An Introduction to Reader-Response Criticism." In *Reader-Response Theory: From Formalism to Post-Structuralism*, edited by Jane P. Tompkins, ix–xxi. Baltimore MD: Johns Hopkins University Press, 1980.

———. "The Reader in History: The Changing Shape of Literary Response." In *Reader-Response Theory: From Formalism to Post-Structuralism*, edited by Jane P. Tompkins, 201–32. Baltimore MD: Johns Hopkins University Press, 1980.

Trudeau, Garry. "Death and Politics on the Funny Pages: Garry Trudeau Addresses American Newspaper Editors." *Critical Studies in Media Communication* 24, no. 1 (2007): 86–89.

Walker, Brian. *The Comics: The Complete Collection*. New York: Abrams Press, 2011.

Wanzo, Rebecca. *The Content of Our Caricature*. New York: NYU Press, 2020.

———. "It's a Hero? Black Comics and Satirizing Subjection." In *The Blacker the Ink: Constructions of Black Identity in Comics and Sequential Art*, edited by Frances Gateward and John Jennings, 314–32. New Brunswick NJ: Rutgers University Press, 2015.

Watterson, Bill. "The Bill Watterson Interview." By Richard Samuel West. *Comics Journal*, no. 127 (March 1989). http://www.tcj.com/the-bill -watterson-interview.

Watterson, Bill, and Jenny Robb. *Exploring "Calvin and Hobbes": An Exhibition Catalog*. Kansas City MO: Andrews McMeel Publishing, 2015.

White, Sylvia E., and Tania Fuentez. "Analysis of Black Images in Comic Strips, 1915–1995." *Newspaper Research Journal* 18, no. 12 (1997): 72–78.

INDEX

comics creators, 2–12, 16, 19–20, 23–24, 27–29, 32, 34, 39, 42–47, 50–52, 55–57, 62–63, 65–66, 69–73, 76–77, 83–89, 91–92, 109, 111–12, 115, 120–22, 132, 137, 142, 146–47, 151, 153; as flexible, 18, 24, 40, 73, 128; persona of, 4, 24, 27, 39, 42–43, 54, 55–62, 66, 69, 72–73, 78, 122–23

Comics Kingdom, 2, 41, 83

comics layout: diegetic space in, 17–18, 53, 75, 109, 116–17, 127, 131–32, 138; style of, 37–38, 49, 52–53; techniques of, 43, 78

comics production and creation: as career, 2–3, 5, 12–13, 18, 40–43; and flexible materialism, 14, 17–19, 22, 52; history and development of, 7, 19–20, 51, 156; and "ideal life," 8, 22–23, 165n72; and isolation vs. everyday life, 22–23; material conditions of, 12, 49, 124; precarity of, 3, 42, 155–56; processes of, 2, 105; racial and gender barriers of, 6–9; syndicate model vs. flexible model of, 13. *See also* technology

comics studies, 6, 19, 123

commodity culture, 51, 68, 71, 73–74; and advertisements, 12, 20, 49–51, 55, 103; and branding, 3, 28, 49–57, 88, 124; and merchandise, 3, 11–13, 24, 39–40, 51, 55–56, 71

"confidence culture," 43, 60, 123

Coole, Diana, 21, 90, 109, 129

COVID-19 pandemic, 39, 47, 143, 146, 151, 153–54, 158

critical race literary criticism, 31–32, 111–12

Cyree, Tia T. M., 108

Dagbovie-Mullins, Sika, 110

Descartes, René, 20

Dinnen, Zara, 124–25

Family Circus (comic) (Keane), 5, 69, 140

Fies, Brian, 21

flexible comics, 3, 15, 18–20, 24–25, 27, 44–45, 47, 57, 79, 98, 113, 120–21, 128, 130, 132, 143, 153

flexible materialism, 14, 17–19, 22, 52

Fritzi Ritz (comic) (Whittington), 7, 70, 84, 87–88, 90

Frost, Samantha, 21, 90, 109, 129

Fruhlinger, Josh, 151, 153

Fuentez, Tania, 101, 108

Gateward, Frances, 6, 104–5

gender, 7, 29, 43–44, 83, 86, 94; as identity, 32, 90, 101–2, 112; as socially constructed, 33, 90, 99, 112–13; and traditional gender roles, 93; as transgender, 89, 153

Gilchrist, Guy, 72, 78, 87

GoComics, 2, 9, 11, 18, 41, 47, 53, 74, 83, 98, 129

Goldstein, Nancy, 6

Gordon, Ian, 19, 50–51, 71, 163n1

Griffith, Bill, 85; *Zippy the Pinhead*, 85

Groensteen, Thierry, 36–37

Guynes, Sean, 26

Haraway, Donna, 26

Harman, Graham, 20, 46, 125–26, 133

Harrington, Oliver, 6

Harris, Malcolm, 28, 56

Hatfield, Charles, 1–2, 14, 69; *Alternative Comics*, 1–2, 14, 69

Hearst, William Randolph, 1, 72, 88

Heer, Jeet, 7

Milton Keynes UK
Ingram Content Group UK Ltd.
UKHW011813110823
426631UK00016B/217

9 781496 235862